HANDCRAFTED PROJECTS

FOR YOUR HOME

56 Make-It-Yourself Accessories to PERSONALIZE Your Space

JERRI FARRIS AND TIM HIMSEL

Creative Publishing
international

CHANHASSEN, MINNESOTA
www.creativepub.com

CONTENTS

Introduction
page 4

PROJECTS

Introduction

Welcome to *Handcrafted Projects for the Home.* In these pages, we're going to explore creative, sometimes remarkable, ways to infuse your home with personality and style. This is a book for those who prefer "handcrafted" over "mass produced"; those who appreciate character and charm; or those who simply enjoy making things that can be used and enjoyed by their families and friends.

We've filled the book with step-by-step instructions for sensational furnishings and accessories you can make yourself. Many of the projects start with items from flea markets, garage sales and antique and thrift stores. Others are based on inexpensive materials that can be found in home centers everywhere. All of them are affordable.

The projects were designed with ordinary people in mind. You don't have to be a fine woodworker or have years of experience to bring these ideas to life. All you really need is some time and the willingness to try.

Whether you're a beginner or a seasoned pro, you're sure to find ideas that send you scurrying to the garage or workshop. To simplify the process, we've broken the projects down into manageable steps and deliberately constructed things in the simplest ways we know. We've also included a chapter with additional information on techniques that may not be familiar to you.

So, come on along. Let us show you what happens when you combine simple materials and inspiration with a sense of adventure and a whole lot of fun.

As you look through the projects and read the directions in this book, you'll notice that they often begin with "salvaged" materials. This is a polite term. The truth is, the materials for these projects were gathered from all kinds of places, some of them pretty unlikely sources for treasures.

If you're not already a seasoned veteran, allow us to introduce you to the fine art of scrounging.

Start by looking through your own attic, basement, garage, or other storage areas where you might have stashed items that could be refurbished or adapted to other uses. It helps to look at old things with new eyes, trying to see not so much what they are as what they could be. When you've been through the nooks and crannies of your own home, branch out to the homes of family and friends.

Tell people about your interest in old things and volunteer to help clean out storage areas any time you get the chance. You never know what might turn up in someone's attic or basement during spring cleaning or when they're packing to move.

If you see something you're interested in at a curb or in a Dumpster, don't be shy. It's polite to ask first, but most people consider anything that has obviously been discarded as trash to be fair game. There are treasures to be had simply by keeping a sharp eye out and being brave.

Shop estate and garage sales, flea markets, junk stores, and salvage yards. Watch for annual neighborhood garage sales, which can offer lots of selection within one stop. Classified ads that include the words "moving sale" or something like "40 year's accumulation" promise great possibilities.

At sales of all sorts, timing is everything. There's no way around it—if you want the best selection, you have to get there first. Although many people do it, we don't recommend knocking on doors before sales actually begin. A little consideration is in order, even when there are treasures at stake. Make sure you arrive at promising garage sales at least fifteen minutes before the sale is scheduled to start.

We find that people gather very early for estate sales. In many regions, the custom is that the first person in line hands

out numbers to those who follow. In some cases there's a common agreement that people can go have coffee or a nap and then return to line in order of their original appearance. In other situations, it's understood that you have to be present to hold your place in line.

If you're not sure about the procedure, ask someone who appears to be a regular. Believe me, bargain hunters can be fiercely protective, and you don't want to start the day with a disagreement over who gets the first look at the loot.

Arriving early is a good strategy, but being there at the end of a sale has advantages as well. People who organize estate sales often make arrangements for a Dumpster to be delivered on sale day. When the sale closes, many things that didn't sell get tossed. If you're on hand when that process begins, you might find treasures free for the ask-

ing. If you offer to help, you're almost sure to be given the green light to take a few things that interest you.

The same sort of idea works with garage sales. People often give their garage sale leftovers to charitable organizations. At the end of a sale, introduce yourself and offer to help organize or cart away whatever remains—you might strike gold.

In many communities, there is another, intriguing source of treasures: giveaway bulletin boards on the Internet. These "free markets," designed to promote recycling and reduce the strain on the waste management system, are operated as a public service. People list and describe unwanted items, which are offered free to the first person to claim and remove them. The system is remarkably simple and effective. Log on—you won't believe what great stuff is available.

FLEA MARKET GUIDELINES

- DRESS COMFORTABLY, IN LAYERS IF THE WEATHER COULD BE VARIABLE. PACK A SMALL BACKPACK WITH SUNGLASSES, A HAT, BOTTLED WATER, AND SUNBLOCK.
- BRING CASH IN SMALL DENOMINATIONS. MANY DEALERS ACCEPT CHECKS OR EVEN CREDIT CARDS, BUT IT'S ALMOST ALWAYS EASIER TO GET THE BEST PRICE IF YOU'RE OFFERING CASH.
- BRING ROOM DIMENSIONS (IF YOU'RE SHOPPING FOR FURNITURE), A TAPE MEASURE, A SMALL NOTEBOOK, AND A PEN.
- IF YOU'RE LOOKING FOR COLLECTIBLES, BRING APPROPRIATE PRICE GUIDES, A MAGNIFYING GLASS, AND A SMALL FLASHLIGHT.
- BRING THE LARGEST VEHICLE YOU HAVE, AND STOCK IT WITH BOXES OR BAGS; PADDING; AND STRING, ROPE, OR BUNGEE CORDS.

For many treasure hunters, flea markets are the mother of all sources, the big kahuna, the reason for getting up early on weekend mornings. If you're already a seasoned pro, you already know how to "work a flea." If not, read on, McDuff.

The first thing you need to know is how to find the good ones. If you're going to operate locally for the most part, start with regional newspapers and trade journals for antiques dealers. If your adventures take on a wider range, check out one of the many flea market guides available at libraries and bookstores.

You'll quickly discover that some markets operate every week, year-round; some have schedules that change with the seasons; others take place only two or three times each year. Pick a couple of likely spots and make some plans! It may be as simple as meeting friends across town on a Saturday morning or as complex as a cross-country road trip.

Experienced flea market fanatics usually start early and stay late or come back at the end of the show. In the early hours, dealers and professional "pickers" often comb the booths for the best pieces. At the end of the show, if a piece you want is still available, you might get a better price from a weary dealer who doesn't want to pack it back up.

When you first get started, everything in every display will draw your attention, and it will take a long time to move from booth to booth. After a while, you'll figure out the types of pieces that lend themselves to projects and how to spot the dealers who are likely to offer them. Sometimes a quick scan of a booth tells all, and other times you'll need to dig under layers of extraneous bits and pieces to find the treasures waiting there. Follow your instincts—they'll lead you to the good stuff.

If you're a bargain hunter at heart, you probably have your own style of negotiating. If not, practice this phrase: "Is this the best you can do?" Or, try this one: "Can you do better?" These are standard ways of asking for a lower price, and dealers will often come down 10 percent or so in reply. Be realistic. You don't want to pay too much, but you don't want to insult a dealer to the point that he or she won't negotiate, either.

Before making a final decision, carefully check out the item's condition. Look for signs of damage, repair, or alteration. Such things rarely matter when you're looking for project materials, but that should be a decision rather than an oversight. For one thing, you don't want to pay the price for a piece in mint condition if it's actually cracked or damaged.

Above all, be guided by your heart. If something speaks to you, listen. If you feel yourself settling for something that's merely acceptable, walk away. Spectacular projects come only from the things that genuinely call to you.

ℬACKDROPS

Backdrops—the walls, windows, doors, and floors—provide the scale and the boundaries for a room. They also provide excellent opportunities to have fun with projects.

Let's start with the walls. You can use special techniques to provide texture or even decoration through murals and trompe l'oeil (see page 23). Be fearless. The materials you'll need for wall projects are inexpensive and easy to change with the seasons and the decor.

Windows and doors can be dressed for success, too. The treatments don't need to be expensive or difficult to construct. Even something as ordinary as copper pipe can become extraordinary with a little time and effort (see page 16).

And don't forget the floors. We haven't. The simple techniques we use for making a floor cloth can be mastered in an afternoon. We provide an interesting pattern (see page 14), but there's no reason to limit yourself to reproducing our ideas. Start there and branch out in any direction that suits your tastes, personality, and decorating style.

Backdrops offer opportunities to express yourself, to create rooms that reflect your family's unique stories and histories. As you look through the projects shown here, think about what you can use to make your home more personal.

VINYL FLOOR CLOTH

Bring a Native American theme into a room with
an inexpensive, durable floor cloth.

*1 Cut a 36 × 60" (91.44 cm × 1.52 m) piece of vinyl.
Roll a coat of latex-based primer onto the back of the vinyl.
When the primer is dry, paint the entire floor cloth with
two coats of the base paint.*

*2 Mark the horizontal and vertical centers of the floor
cloth, and transfer the pattern (shown on page 183) onto
it. Mask off the edges of the center medallion; seal the
inside edges of the tape with matte medium, and let it dry.
(This keeps the paint from seeping under the tape when
you paint.)*

*3 Paint the center sections of the medallion, let the
paint dry, and remove the tape. Continue masking and
painting one color at a time until the pattern is complete.
Let the paint dry for a week, then add two coats of water-
based polyurethane.*

MATERIALS:

• SCRAP OF SHEET VINYL • LATEX-BASED PRIMER
• MASKING TAPE • MATTE MEDIUM
• ACRYLIC PAINT • WATER-BASED POLYURETHANE

DOORKNOB DRAPERY

Draw the view into the rooms with these imaginative window treatments.

Note: for windows wider than 40" (1 m), support the rod with three doorknobs.

1 Loosen the setscrew and remove the stem from each knob. Use two-part epoxy to glue a knob into each escutcheon.

2 Locate the studs near the outside edges of the window. Hold each escutcheon in position, mark and drill pilot holes, and use 2" (5 cm) brass screws to hang it. If there are no studs in suitable locations, use wall anchors to support the weight.

3 Cut two pieces of silk cord, each about 30" (75 cm) long. Tie a knot 2" (5 cm) above the bottom of each cord; fray the cord below the knot. String beads onto the cord, stacking them to about 4½" (11 cm). Make loops in the cord and hold them in place with several twists of 16-gauge (1.5 mm) copper wire. Stack another inch or two (2.5 to 5 cm) of beads, and knot the cord again. Cut a piece of copper pipe about 16" (40 cm) longer than the window is wide. Glue an end cap to each end of the pipe, then set it on top of the door-knobs. Arrange your fabric or drapes over the pipe and allow it to hang down the sides of the window. Tie the beaded cord to the pipe, between the doorknob and the window trim. Add a brass finial to the endcap, if desired.

MATERIALS:

- ANTIQUE DOORKNOBS AND ESCUTCHEONS
- TWO-PART EPOXY • 2" (5 CM) BRASS SCREWS (4)
- 16-GAUGE (1.5 MM) COPPER WIRE • ½" (12 MM) RIGID COPPER PIPE
- ½" (12 MM) END CAPS (2) • BRASS FINIALS (OPTIONAL)
- 2 YARDS (1.8 M) OF SATIN DRAPERY CORD • BEADS

MOSAIC TILE ALCOVE

Add architectural details above windows or doors.

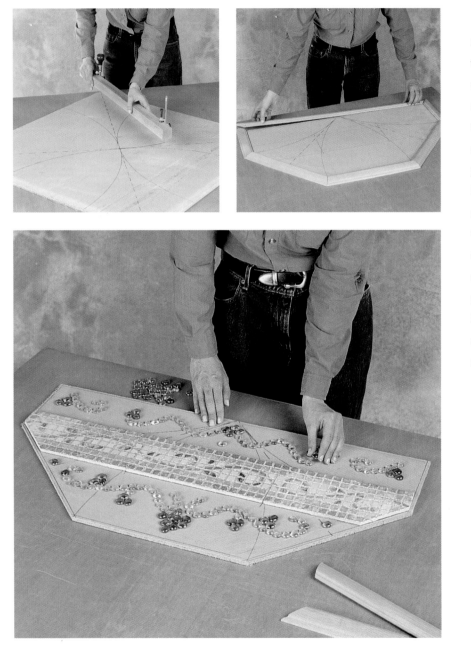

1 Measure the window and cut a square of cementboard to match its width. Draw diagonal lines from corner to corner, forming an X across the square. Set a compass to the distance between one corner and the center of the X. With the point of the compass at each corner in turn, draw a series of arcs that intersect the sides of the square. Connect those points to make an octagon shape. Draw a center line dividing the square into two equal parts. Score and cut the cementboard at the center line; score and cut extra corner triangles to form the shape of the pediment.

(continued on page 20)

MATERIALS:

- CEMENTBOARD • TRIM BOARDS
- PAINT OR STAIN • CERAMIC TILE
- THIN-SET MORTAR • GLASS STONES
- HOT GLUE • GROUT
- 2" (5 CM) DRYWALL SCREWS

(continued from page 19)

2 *Measure each side of the cementboard and cut trim boards to match, mitering the corners. Paint or stain the pieces and set them aside.*

3 *Lay out the border tile and mark them for cutting. Use a wet saw or tile cutter to cut the tile to fit. Set the tile in place and draw placement lines on the cementboard. Follow the pattern and mark the design onto the cementboard, or create your own design to complement the tile you've selected. Spread thin-set mortar on the cementboard and set the tile. To set the tile, wrap a short piece of 2 × 4 (5 × 10 cm) in scrap carpeting or a towel. Lay this block over the tile and tap it lightly with a rubber mallet. Let the mortar dry, according to manufacturer's instructions. Use hot glue to attach decorative glass stones to the marked design, then let the glue cool.*

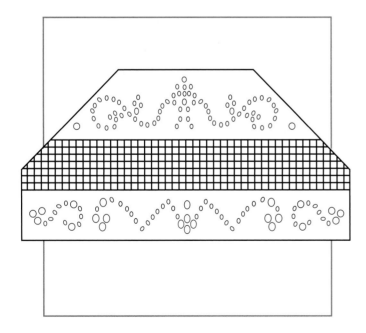

◀4▶ Locate the studs in the wall above the window. Hold the cementboard in position and mark the stud locations onto it. Drill two or three pilot holes along each marked location, then screw the pediment into position on the wall, using 2" (5 cm) drywall screws.

◀5▶ Mix latex fortifier into sanded grout. Apply the grout to the pediment, using a sponge to fill the areas surrounding the glass stones, and a grout float to fill the joints between the border tile. Wipe away excess grout with a damp sponge. Let the grout dry for an hour, then polish away the powdery haze with a dry cloth.

◀6▶ Carefully position the trim pieces at the edges of the cementboard and secure them with construction adhesive. Tape the trim boards in place until the construction adhesive dries completely.

PAINTED CHARMS

Create a custom trompe l'oeil design by repeating a design motif from
window treatments or upholstery fabrics.

1 *Trace the design, then use a photocopier to enlarge
or reduce the drawing to produce a pattern.*

2 *Put a piece of graphite paper behind the pattern,
and trace the design onto the wall. Use a dull pencil or a
stylus, and be careful not to smudge or tear the paper as
you work.*

3 *Following the colors and shading of the fabric pattern you're reproducing, paint the design.*

MATERIALS:

• TRACING PAPER • GRAPHITE PAPER
• DULL PENCIL OR STYLUS • ACRYLIC PAINT

DOORKNOB HANGERS

Intricate old doorknobs add interesting texture to simple projects.
Here are two good ideas.

Hanger Board: *Drill pilot holes in a piece of reclaimed lumber and install a hanger bolt in each. Remove the stems from the doorknobs, either by unscrewing the knob, loosening the setscrew, or cutting the stem with a hacksaw. Attach each knob to a hanger bolt, and then add hanging hardware to the back of the board.*

Door Hanger: *Remove the stem from the doorknob as described above. Mark and drill a pilot hole, and install a hanger bolt on a door or wall. If you're installing the bolt on a wall, be sure you hit a stud or use appropriate hardware. Attach the escutcheon, then screw the door- knob onto the hanger bolt.*

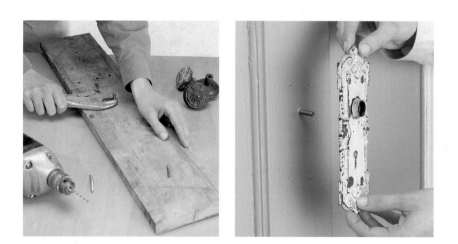

MATERIALS:
• Doorknobs and escutcheons • Hanger bolts (1 per knob)
• Reclaimed lumber • Hanging hardware

RIBBON BOARD

A ribbon board provides attractive display space for mementos and souvenirs.

1 Remove the mirror from its mirror frame. Clean, sand, and paint the frame. Measure the opening and cut a piece of ⅜" (9 mm) plywood to fit.

2 Cut quilt batting 2" (5 cm) larger than the plywood; cut fabric 3" (7.5 cm) larger. Layer the fabric (right-side down), the batting, and the plywood. Wrap the batting and fabric around the plywood, keeping the grain straight and the fabric taut; staple the fabric in place.

3 Arrange the ribbons, pull them taut, and tack them in place. Cut each ribbon to extend about 1" (2.5 cm) beyond the fabric on the back, then turn the board over and staple them in place.

4 Insert a tack at selected intersections, then hot glue a button to each tack. Toenail the finished board into the mirror frame. Add hanging hardware.

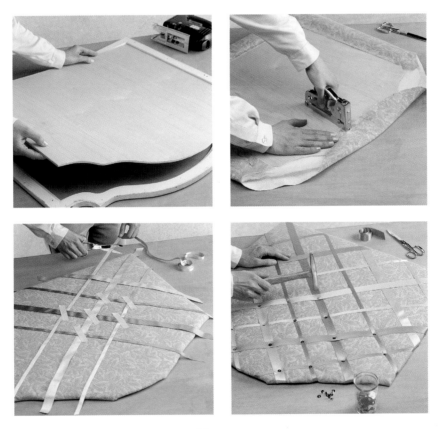

MATERIALS:

• MIRROR FRAME • LATEX PAINT • ⅜" (9 MM) PLYWOOD • QUILT BATTING • FABRIC • RIBBONS
• TACKS • ANTIQUE BUTTONS • HOT GLUE • HANGING HARDWARE

MESSAGE CENTER

Blackboard paint and brass coat hooks turn a salvaged door panel into an attractive, functional message center.

1 Cut the door panel to size. If you like, remove the old finish and sand the entire piece. Mask off the center panel, then stain and apply a finish to the rails and stiles.

2 When the finish is completely dry, mask off the rails and stiles, and apply several coats of blackboard paint to the center panel.

3 Add brass hooks along the bottom rail, and an escutcheon and doorknob to the stile on one side.

MATERIALS:

• PANEL DOOR • BLACKBOARD PAINT • BRASS HOOKS (3)
• DOORKNOB AND ESCUTCHEON PLATE

KEEPSAKE CLOTHING

Showcase heirloom clothing in a vintage domed-glass frame.

1 *Disassemble the frame. Using the original as a template, cut a foam board. (If the original isn't available, cut a board ¼" [6 mm] smaller than the frame opening.)*

2 *Cut a piece of fabric 2" (5 cm) larger than the mounting board. Cover the foam board with spray adhesive, then wrap the fabric around it. Tape the edges of the fabric to the back of the board.*

3 *Attach the items to the mounting board. Support clothing with three or four strategically placed hand stitches, then bring the threads to the back, tie the tails, and secure them. Use silicone glue to hold other items in place. Set the mounting board in the frame and insert ¾" (19 mm) brads into the center of each side, then*

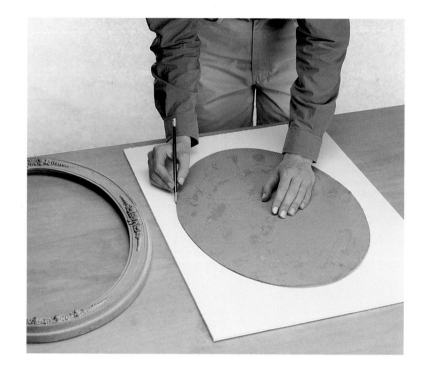

the top and bottom. Insert additional brads at about 2" (5 cm) intervals. Cover the frame back with brown paper, using double-stick transfer tape. Replace the hanging hardware.

MATERIALS:

- FRAME WITH DOMED GLASS • ACID-FREE FOAM BOARD
- ARCHIVIST'S SPRAY ADHESIVE • FRAMER'S TAPE
- SILICONE GLUE • ¾" (19 MM) BRADS
- BROWN PAPER • DOUBLE-STICK TRANSFER TAPE
- HANGING HARDWARE

COAT RACK

Home is where you hang your hat … or your jacket!

1 *Find the studs in the wall, and if possible, plan to center the coat rack over a stud. Decide how long the coat rack will be and cut a birch log to fit. (We made ours 48" [1.22 m].) Mark a straight line along the length of each side of the log, and use a circular saw to cut along those marks. If necessary, complete the cut with a handsaw.*

2 *Starting 4" (10.16 cm) from one end, mark and drill evenly spaced ¼" holes for the pegs. Cut the ¾" dowel into pegs, one for each hole. Sand the pegs, rounding over the edges of the ends, and glue one into each hole. Finish the pegs and the faces of the pine buttons to match or complement the coat rack. Apply two coats of polyurethane to the entire piece, front and back, if desired.*

3 *Drill a ⅜" (9.5 mm) hole 2" in from each end of the rack and one in the center. Drill corresponding pilot holes in the wall. Insert a hollow wall anchor into any pilot hole that does not hit a stud. Hold the coat rack against the wall. At each ⅜" hole, drive a 3" drywall screw through the log and into the wall. Tap the pine buttons into the holes to cover the screwheads.*

MATERIALS:

BIRCH LOG • ¾" (19.1 CM) PINE DOWEL
PINE BUTTONS • WOOD GLUE • PAINT OR STAIN (OPTIONAL)
SATIN-FINISH POLYURETHANE • 3" (7.62 CM) DRYWALL SCREWS

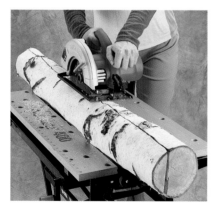

ℐHELVES & 𝒟ISPLAYS

No matter what the object may be or how many memories are attached to it, if it's hidden in a drawer or closet, it's just stuff. Even treasured family photographs are little more than clutter if they're moldering in old shoeboxes at the back of the coat closet. On the other hand, anything from a child's art project to Grandpa's pocketwatch becomes art when it's displayed with style.

Interesting shelves and bookcases are the heart of stylish displays. They're also the heart of this chapter. In the next few pages, you'll find directions for display pieces that are created from scratch, by combining vintage and new pieces, and by embellishing existing pieces. There are shelves, bookcases, cabinets—even a ladder. You'll see that, approached with imagination and a sense of adventure, display pieces can be fashioned from a wide variety of materials.

As you look at the projects in the next few pages, take note of the details. Scrolled wrought-iron brackets transform a rustic door; a mirrored panel reflects items displayed on a small shelf; sumptuous fabric dresses the interior of a vintage armoire. Details like this elevate projects from ordinary to inspired—look for opportunities to include transformative details in your projects.

DISPLAY SHELF

Dress a simple shelf in Victorian-style gingerbread.

1 Cut the parts as indicated below. Miter the corners of the side and front trim. Spread wood glue over the surface of one of the shelf supports, clamp the second shelf support to it, and let the glue dry. Attach the shelf back to the shelf supports with screws driven about every 6" (155 mm). (See diagram on page 185.)

2 Spread glue along the top of the shelf back and the top of the shelf support. Position this assembly over the shelf and attach it with screws driven every 6".

3 Run a bead of Liquid Nails along the first 1½" (40 cm) and corners of the front and side trim, and clamp it in place. Drive a screw through the shelf and into the trim about every 6" along the front and sides. When the adhesive is dry, prime and paint the shelf as desired. Add sturdy hanging hardware.

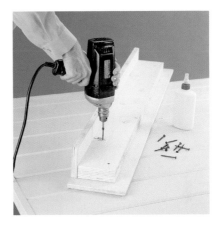

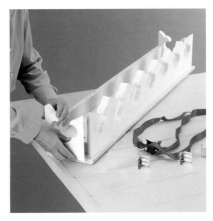

Part	Size	Number
Solid-core veneer plywood:		
Shelf	6½ × 43" (165 × 1090 mm)	1
Shelf supports	4¼ × 40" (110 × 1020 mm)	2
Shelf back	3½ × 40" (90 × 1020 mm)	1
Decorative trim:		
Side trim	6" (155 mm)	2
Front trim	42" (1070 mm)	1

Note: These dimensions are for decorative trim with a 6" repeat, such as this scalloped molding (part # MLD640-8) from Architectural Products by Outwater Industries. (See page 189 for details.)

MATERIALS:

- ½" (12 MM) SOLID-CORE VENEER PLYWOOD
- DECORATIVE TRIM (8 FT. [2400 MM]) • WOOD GLUE
- 1½" (35 MM) WOOD SCREWS • LIQUID NAILS
- LATEX PAINT

CORBEL SHELF

In a foyer or entryway, a vintage corbel topped by a
simple shelf greets guests in style.

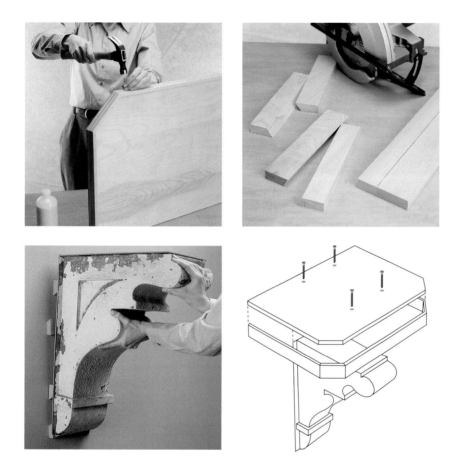

• CORBEL • ¾" (19 MM) AB INTERIOR PLYWOOD • OGEE MOLDING • WOOD GLUE
• 4D FINISH NAILS • 2" (5 CM) WOOD SCREWS • PAINT OR STAIN • PINE 1 × 4 (2.5 × 10 CM)

1 Cut a piece of ¾" (19 mm) plywood
for the top. (The dimensions will depend
on the size of the corbel you're using. We
made ours 32 × 20" [80 × 50 cm]). Trim
the edges of the corners as shown. Cut
ogee molding to fit the top, mitering the
corners. Glue and tack molding along the
front and sides of the shelftop. Paint or
finish the top to match or complement
your corbel.

2 Mark a line down the 1 × 4 (2.5 ×
10 cm), 1⅜" (34 mm) from the long edge.
Set the bevel on a circular saw to 45° and
cut along the marked line. Reset the bevel
on the circular saw to 90° and cut two
pairs of mating cleats to match the width
of your corbel. Use 2" (5 cm) screws to
attach two cleats to the back of the
corbel—one near the top and the other
near the lower edge.

3 Hold the corbel in place and mark
the locations for the mating cleats. Screw
the cleats to the wall. Be sure you hit a
stud or use hollow wall anchors to support the weight.

4 Set the shelftop in place; drill two
counterbored pilot holes through it and
down into the corbel. Secure the top to
the corbel with 2" (5 cm) screws. Fill the
holes and touch up the paint.

PICKET FENCE SHELF

A display piece made from prefab shelves and a section of picket fence
lends a romantic, cottage style to a room.

1 *Buy a section of standard picket fence and cut it
to size. Or, if you prefer a picket style that's not available prefabricated, you can cut your own pickets and
stringers and build a fence section.*

2 *Paint both sides and top and bottom of the fence
section, the brackets, and the shelves with a coat of
latex paint. When that's completely dry, add a coat of
crackle medium. When the crackle medium is dry, add
another coat of latex paint—cracks will appear as the
paint dries.*

3 *Center each shelf on the fence section; mark the
placement of the brackets. Drive screws into the pickets and then attach the brackets to the front of the
fence. Add hanging hardware to the back, hang the
unit, and set the shelves in place.*

Note: When you hang the shelf, drive screws into the
wall studs or use hollow wall anchors to support the
weight of the shelf.

MATERIALS:
• SECTION OF PICKET FENCE • LATEX PAINT (2 COLORS)
• CRACKLE MEDIUM • PREFAB SHELF WITH BRACKETS
• 1" (2.5 CM) DRYWALL SCREWS • HANGING HARDWARE

MIRRORED DOOR SHELF

With a mirror and a few finishing touches, an old door can become an elegant accent for a hallway, entry, or living room.

  1 *Remove the center panels from the top third of the door. (Drill starter holes, make cuts with a jigsaw, and then pull the pieces from the frame.) Restore or refinish the door, if you wish.*

  2 *Have a mirror cut to fit the opening. Set the mirror into the opening and secure it with glazier's points. Drill pilot holes and attach a shelf bracket to the door, centered just below the opening. Set the shelf into place. Attach the door to the wall with cleats (see page 45) or heavy-duty hanging hardware.*

MATERIALS:

• SALVAGED DOOR • MIRROR, CUSTOM CUT
• SHELF BRACKET • GLAZIER'S POINTS

BOOKSHELVES

Make unique shelves from a vintage door and some interesting brackets.

1 *Cut a piece of 2 × 4 6" (15.24 cm) shorter than the width of the door you've selected. Mark a line on the board, 1⅜" (3.49 cm) from the long edge. Set the bevel on a circular saw to 45° and cut along the marked line. Cut the pieces into two sets of cleats. Use 2½" drywall screws to attach the cleats to the back of the door, with the angled point facing down, one at the top and one at the bottom. Hold the door in place and mark the wall at the location of the mating cleats. Screw the cleats to the wall, with the angled point facing up. Be sure you hit a stud or use hollow wall anchors designed to support the combined weight of the door and bookshelves.*

2 *Determine the placement, size, and number of shelves that are appropriate for your door. (We used two.) Cut 1 × 12 lumber to size and rout the edges of each shelf, using an ogee bit. Finish the shelves to match or complement the door and let them dry.*

Mark placement lines for the shelves and for the brackets, marking brackets below each shelf, 2" (5.08 cm) from each end. Drill pilot holes, and attach the brackets beneath the placement lines for the shelves, using ¾" drywall screws. Put the shelves in place, drill pilot holes, and attach the brackets to the shelves. Attach the book shelf to the wall.

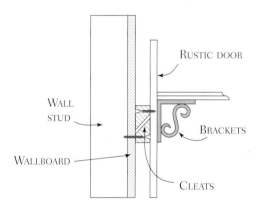

RUSTIC DOOR

WALL STUD

WALLBOARD

BRACKETS

CLEATS

MATERIALS:

• RUSTIC DOOR • 2 × 4 (5.08 × 10.16 CM) • 2½" (6.35 CM) DRYWALL SCREWS • WROUGHT-IRON BRACKETS (2 PER SHELF)
• 1 × 12 (2.54 × 30.48 CM) FINISH-GRADE LUMBER • PAINT OR STAIN AND WATER-BASED, SATIN-FINISH POLYURETHANE
• ¾" (19.1 MM) DRYWALL SCREWS

EMBELLISHED BOOKCASE

Give cottage character to a basic bookcase by adding interesting details.

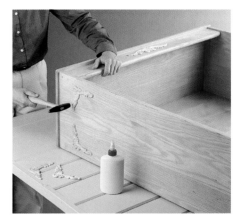

1 Sand the bookcase as necessary. Arrange the wood appliques and attach them according to the manufacturer's directions. (We drilled pilot holes and secured the appliques with wood glue and finish nails.) Prime the entire bookcase, inside and out, and let it dry. Paint the exterior and let it dry. Apply wallpaper sizing to the interior and let it dry, following the manufacturer's instructions. To give them more depth, paint the wood appliques with double-strength coffee or tea.

2 Tear butcher paper into irregularly shaped pieces no larger than 6 × 6" (150 × 150 mm). Leave straight edges on some pieces for the top and bottom of the bookcase. Mix water and paint in a ratio of about 4:1. Wearing rubber gloves, dip a piece of paper into the paint mixture; hold it up and let most of the paint drip away. Gently crumple the paper, then flatten it on a plastic-covered surface and let it dry. Experiment with the amount that you crumple the paper and adjust the water-to-paint ratio until you get the effect you want. The paint will settle into the creases, so the more you crumple the paper, the more veins of color it will have.

3 Roll wallpaper adhesive onto both sides of a piece of prepared paper and paste it in place, smoothing the wrinkles outward from the center on each side with a wallpaper brush. Start with the straight-edged pieces at the top and bottom, then fill in the open areas with irregularly shaped pieces. Overlap the edges slightly; add pieces in alternating areas to allow each piece some time to dry before adding an overlapping piece. Smooth each piece to squeeze out any excess paste and remove any air bubbles. Rinse the brush as often as necessary to remove the excess paste. When the piece is completely dry, spray the interior with acrylic sealer.

Note: Practice by papering a scrap of foam core or plywood before working on the bookcase.

MATERIALS:

• PREFAB BOOKCASE • DECORATIVE WOOD APPLIQUES • WOOD GLUE
• 4D (38 MM) FINISH NAILS • LATEX PRIMER • LATEX PAINT
• UNCOATED WHITE BUTCHER PAPER • WALLPAPER SIZING • WALLPAPER ADHESIVE
• SPRAY ACRYLIC SEALER

REFURBISHED CABINET

Lining the inside walls and shelves on a vintage armoire or cabinet freshens
the look without damaging the original finish.

1 ▷ Remove the shelves and shelf supports. Cut a piece of foam board ¼" (6 mm) smaller than the length and width of the back of the cabinet. Use spray adhesive to attach an over-sized piece of quilt batting to the foam board; trim the batting to fit.

2 ▷ Cut a piece of fabric, 4" (10 cm) larger than the foam board. Set the foam board—fleece-side down—onto the back side of the fabric. Wrap the fabric around the foam board and glue it down as necessary. Press pieces of self-adhesive hook-and-loop tape onto the corners and sides of the back of the cabinet and the foam board. Position the foam board on the back of the cabinet, pressing it firmly to secure the hook-and-loop tape.

3 ▷ Wrap each shelf in fabric; glue the overlapped fabric at the back edge. Replace the shelf supports and shelves. Measure and cut foam board to fit the sections of the sides. Cover and install these side pieces, following the instructions above.

MATERIALS:

- CABINET OR ARMOIRE • ACID-FREE FOAM BOARD
- ARCHIVIST'S SPRAY ADHESIVE • QUILT BATTING
- FABRIC • GLUE • SELF-ADHESIVE HOOK-AND-LOOP TAPE

APPLE LADDER

Leaned against a wall, an apple ladder displays quilts, towels, or vintage linens in a bedroom or bathroom.

1 *Cut two 72" (1.8 m) 1 × 4s (2.5 × 10 cm). Mark and cut a 10° angle at one end and an 80° angle at the other of each board. On each board, center a mark 10½" (26 cm) from one end; make four more marks, each one 14" (35 cm) from the other. Using a 1" (2.5 cm) hole saw, cut one hole at each mark.*

2 *Cut five rungs from a 1¼" (3 cm) dowel, 26", 22½", 19¼", 16", and 12½" (65, 56, 48, 40, and 31 cm) long. Arrange the rungs so that the ladder narrows as it reaches the top. Glue the dowels into the holes and tack them into place, angling the nails down through the legs and into the dowels. Paint or stain the ladder as desired.*

MATERIALS:
• PINE 1 × 4S (2.5 × 10 CM) (2) • 1¼" (3 CM) WOOD DOWEL (8 FT. [2.5 M])
• WOOD GLUE • 6D (5 CM) FINISH NAILS • PAINT OR STAIN

$\mathcal{F}$URNISHINGS

Trust us. You can build and create furnishings, even if you're not an experienced, skilled woodworker. Many of the projects in this chapter require no woodworking at all. Those that do were devised with simple construction methods that don't require years of experience or an extensive workshop. Don't let the idea of building furniture intimidate you.

The projects were tested by people with a wide range of abilities and experience, and they're realistic for novices as well as more experienced craftspeople. Pick a favorite project, read through the directions, and entertain the possibilities.

Once you've finished a project, don't settle for using it for only its most obvious purposes. Five-board benches (page 80), for example, work well in entryways as places to rest while changing out of boots or shoes. They can also act as auxiliary seating during parties, as end tables or coffee tables, or even, when stacked on top of one another, as bookshelves. A mirrored tray table (page 70) is a wonderful place to serve light meals or display flower arrangements. With the addition of a simple fabric skirt, an oversized version would make a lovely vanity or dressing table.

You're sure to enjoy making these pieces as well as using them in your home.

DECOUPAGE TABLE

Make any meal a special occasion with this whimsical decoupaged table.

1 From ¾" MDF, cut one 48"-diameter (1220 mm) round tabletop and a table anchor sized to match the arms of your pedestal base. Rout the edges of the tabletop with an ogee bit. Mark the center of the tabletop and of the anchor. Match those centers and attach the anchor to the tabletop, using 1½" screws driven down from the top. Fill the screw holes with lightweight spackle. When dry, lightly sand the spackle. Turn the tabletop over; mark and drill pilot holes on the anchor to match the arms of the pedestal base (as shown at right).

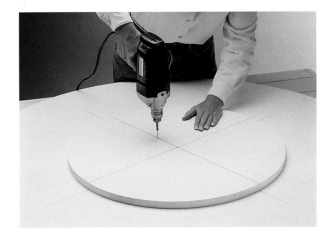

MATERIALS:

• ¾" (19 MM) MDF • 1½" (38 MM) WOOD SCREWS • LIGHTWEIGHT SPACKLE • PRIMER • LATEX PAINT, OFF WHITE • SPRAY GLOSS ENAMEL, GRAY OR TAUPE • LACE FABRIC OR TABLECLOTH • VINTAGE PLATES (4) • VINTAGE SILVERWARE (1 PLACE SETTING) • WHITE GLUE • WATER-BASED POLYURETHANE VARNISH • 2" (5 CM) WOOD SCREWS

2 Prime the tabletop and let it dry; add two coats of off-white paint. Smooth the lace over the top and tape it to the back. Spray an even coat of gray or taupe enamel over the lace, including the edges of the table. Remove the lace when the paint is dry.

3 Make color photocopies of four vintage plates, enlarging each to approximately 12¾" (325 mm). Make color copies of vintage silver—four each of a knife, dinner and dessert fork, and spoon—enlarging each piece by

approximately 25%. Lightly sand the back of each image, then use a pair of small, sharp scissors to cut out each one.

4 ▸ Arrange the images to resemble a table setting, and lightly sand the table in the areas where the images will be placed. Dilute 3 parts of white glue with one part of water and paint it on the back of each image. Gently smooth the paper with a bone press, making sure there are no creases or folds. When the glue is dry, apply five or six coats of water-based polyurethane varnish, letting each coat dry before applying the next. With each coat, alternate between horizontal and vertical brushstrokes. Sand lightly between coats, and remove any dust with tack cloth. Install the pedestal base by driving 2" screws up through the holes in the pedestal and into the anchor and tabletop.

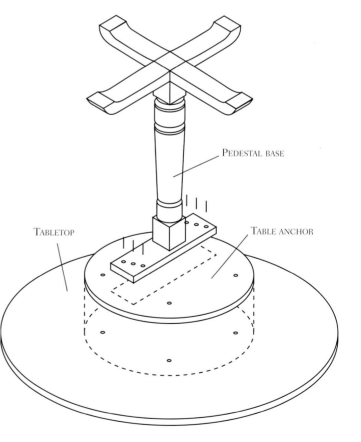

PEDESTAL BASE

TABLETOP

TABLE ANCHOR

BASIC DECOUPAGE TECHNIQUES

To prepare the surface, sand the object until it's smooth, seal it with shellac or pigmented shellac, and let it dry. Lightly sand the coat of shellac and wipe away any dust with tack cloth. Apply two coats of paint and let them dry.

Cut out the images. Start by rough cutting with large scissors, then switch to small scissors to cut along the outside edges of the image. Hold the paper in one hand and turn it as you cut the curves.

Place the image on a cutting mat and use a craft knife to make delicate internal cuts.

Paint the backs of the images with slightly diluted white glue, and reposition them. Press the images down and squeegee them with your fingers to remove any air bubbles or excess glue. Wipe away any excess glue with a damp cloth.

Apply coats of water-based varnish until you're satisfied with the surface. Between coats, let the varnish dry, then sand lightly. Just before adding the next coat of varnish, wipe the surface with tack cloth, taking care to remove all dust.

Apply stain with a paintbrush, then wipe away the excess with a soft, dry cloth, and let it dry. If desired, apply a coat of paste wax and polish the surface.

LEAF TABLE

Top a salvaged base with a handpainted tabletop for an
unusual table for casual dining.

*1▷ Enlarge the pattern below. (Many copy centers
have blueprint copiers and staff members who can help
you reproduce the pattern to scale.) Use a pounce
wheel to transfer the pattern onto the plywood, then
cut out the tabletop. Cut a circle of plywood to match
the diameter of the arms of your pedestal base. Mark
the center of the tabletop and of the plywood circle.
Match those centers and attach the circle to the tabletop with 1½" (4 cm) screws driven down through the*

*top. Fill the screw holes and any voids in the edges of
the plywood with lightweight spackle. When dry, lightly
sand the spackle.*

*2▷ Paint a basecoat onto the table. Add details as
indicated on the pattern.*

*3▷ Install the pedestal base by driving 2" (5 cm)
screws up through the holes in the pedestal and into
the plywood circle and tabletop.*

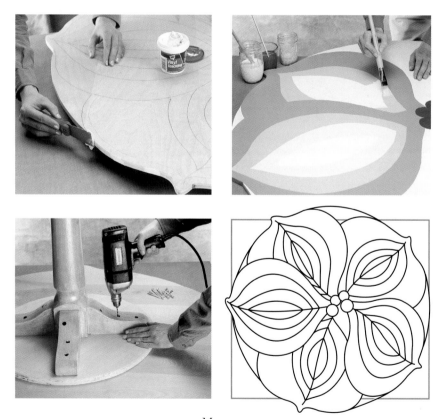

MATERIALS:
• ¾" (19 mm) plywood • 1½" (4 cm) screws • Paints • 2" (5 cm) screws • Pattern
• Table base • Pounce wheel • Spackle

BIRCH TREE TABLE

Transform birch plywood and branches into a fanciful table for your bedside or entryway. (See page 177 for information on harvesting trees for this project.)

1 *Rough-cut two 30" sections of a tree trunk, using a bow saw. Cut the branches to similar lengths, then turn the trunk upside down on a flat work surface. Trim branches until the trunk is stable and nearly vertical. Using a scrap 2 × 4 (5.08 × 10.16 cm) as a gauge, scribe the end of each branch for a plumb cut. Trim the branches with a jigsaw or reciprocating saw.*

2 *Set the trunks back on the level surface, mark a height of 25" (63.5 cm) all the way around each one, and use a reciprocating saw to trim them. Set the trunks together. Experiment with arrangements until the branches are interwoven in an interesting pattern and the tops of the trunks are butted or nearly butted together. Find three or four places where the trunks and branches meet, drill pilot holes, and screw the pieces together, using 3 to 4" drywall screws. If necessary, sand the trunks until the tops are level with one another.*

3 *Cut a 22"-diameter (55.88 cm) circle from the birch plywood. Cut 1"-diameter branches into about 75 pieces, each 2" (5.08 cm) long. Place the tabletop upside down on a level work surface. Spread wood glue along several inches at a time, and tack twigs in place to cover the edge. Place the twig pieces so the tops are flush with the tabletop and the edges are butted together as closely as possible.*

4 *Place the tabletop on the trunks, adjust until the tabletop is stable, then trace the positions of the trunks onto the bottom of the tabletop. Remove the tabletop and drill a pilot hole at the center of the marking for each trunk. Spread wood glue on top of each trunk, replace the tabletop, and fasten it to the base with 2" drywall screws. Fill and sand the holes for the screws. Paint the tabletop a cream color to complement the birch bark, then seal the entire piece with polyurethane varnish, if desired.*

MATERIALS:

• WELL-DRIED, SPREADING TREE TRUNK SECTIONS, APPROXIMATELY 30" (76.2 CM) (2) • 3 TO 4" (7.62 TO 10.16 CM) DRYWALL SCREWS • ¾" (19.1 MM) BIRCH VENEER PLYWOOD • VARIETY OF 1" (2.54 CM) BIRCH BRANCHES • WOOD GLUE • 1" (2.54 CM) BRADS • 2" (5.08 CM) DRYWALL SCREWS • WOOD PUTTY • WATER-BASED, SATIN-FINISH POLYURETHANE

CLAY POT TABLE

Gardeners love garden-themed accents such as this table
made from a stack of clay pots.

1 Mask off the rims of two clean, dry 17" (43 cm) clay pots. Prime the pots and three pot feet and let them dry. On each, brush on a thin coat of umber acrylic paint and let it dry. Dilute some gold acrylic paint with clear glaze and brush it on lightly—let some umber show through. Let the pots dry, then spray acrylic sealer onto the painted portions.

2 To create the mosaic bands, put spare or damaged clay pots into a paper bag and use a rubber mallet to break them. Hot glue the shards and bits of sea glass to the unpainted strip on the pots. When the glue is set, grout the mosaic, using a sponge to push the grout into the open spaces. Wipe away the excess grout, using a damp sponge. Rinse the sponge often and keep wiping until you've removed all the grit. When the grout

dries, polish the surface with a clean, dry cloth.

3 Stack the pots and run a bead of silicone caulk around the edges. Thread washers and a bolt through the drainage holes to connect the pots, then set the column onto the pot feet. Add rubber bumpers and set the glass in place.

MATERIALS:

• MASKING TAPE • 17" (43 CM) CLAY POTS (2) • POT FEET (3) • ACRYLIC PAINT • CLEAR GLAZE
• CLEAR MATTE ACRYLIC SEALER • HOT GLUE • GROUT • SILICONE CAULK
• 2" (5 CM) MACHINE BOLT AND NUT • METAL WASHERS (2)
• RUBBER BUMPERS • GLASS TABLETOP

DROP LEAF TABLE

Borrow the ambience of vintage linens for a small table with big impact.

   1 *Cut all pieces as indicted on the list below. Enlarge and photo-copy the leaf pattern on page 184. Transfer the pattern to each 14 × 24" piece of MDF. Use a jigsaw to cut out the leaves.*

   2 *Apply a coat of primer to both sides of the top, leaves, aprons, and cleats, and let it dry. Add two coats of white paint, allowing the paint to dry between coats. If it's necessary to prime and paint the legs, do that now. When the paint is thoroughly dry, transfer the main pattern to each of the leaves. Paint the design (see Painting Tips on page 67). Add a ⅛" (3 mm) border of pink around the shaped edges of the leaves and the ends of the table. (We used Delta Ceramacoat's Hydrangea Pink, Wedgwood Green, Bungalow Blue, and Mellow Yellow.)*

   3 *Make placement marks on the legs and both sides of the cleats as*

Part	Material	Size	Number
Top	¾" MDF	19 × 24" (480 mm × 610 mm)	1
Leaf	¾" MDF	14 × 24" (350 mm × 610 mm)	2
Aprons and cleats	1 × 4	17" (430 mm)	4

MATERIALS:

• 8 FT. (2400 MM) CLEAR PINE 1 × 4 (19 × 89 MM) • ¾" (19 MM) MDF
• PRIMER • LATEX PAINT • CRAFT PAINT OR PAINT PENS • SALVAGED TABLE
LEGS (4) • #10 2½" (64 MM) WOOD SCREWS • 1¼" (32 MM) DRYWALL
SCREWS • TABLE HINGES (2 PAIRS) • DROP-LEAF SUPPORTS (1 PAIR)

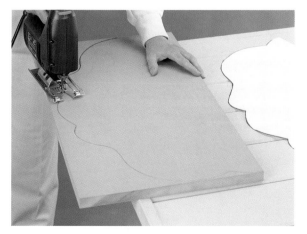

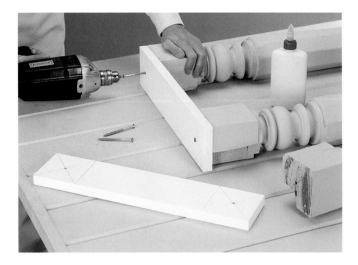

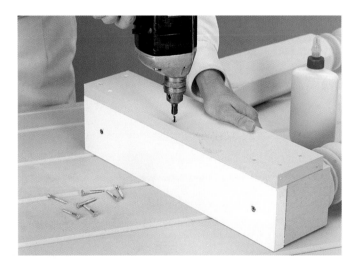

indicated in the diagram below. (Note: Before gluing painted surfaces, use sandpaper to rough up the area to be glued.) Drill pilot holes at placement marks on cleats and legs. Spread wood glue over the tops of the legs. Align a cleat with the legs and attach it to each leg with a 2½" wood screw. Repeat with remaining cleat and pair of legs.

4 Place a cleat/leg assembly on the work surface and position the apron. Spread glue on the edge of the cleat and the face of the legs. Drill pilot holes and screw the apron to the cleat and to the center of each leg, using 1¼" drywall screws. Repeat with remaining cleat/leg assembly and apron.

5 Lay out and mark the cleat positions on the table-top. Spread glue on the cleats, align them on the table, and drill pilot holes. Screw each cleat to the tabletop, using one 1¼" screw near each leg and one in the center.

6 Lay out the tabletop and one leaf on the work surface and use a combination square to mark the

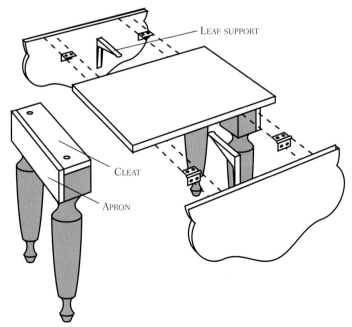

LEAF SUPPORT

CLEAT

APRON

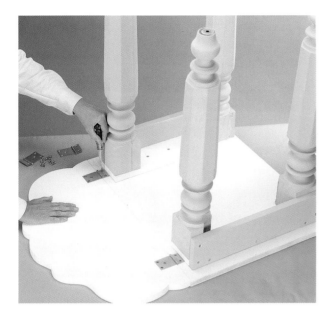

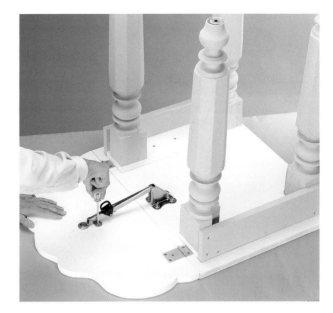

hinge positions. Drill pilot holes and attach the hinges to the leaves, using the screws supplied by the manufacturer. Double-check the alignment of the pieces, then drill pilot holes and screw the hinges to the table-top. (We used brass-plated table hinges from Rockler Woodworking and Hardware, part #29249.)

7 Position a drop leaf support between the cleats

and mark its position. Drill pilot holes, then attach the hardware to the table, using the screws provided by the manufacturer. (We used table drop leaf support #29637 from Rockler.) Follow the manufacturer's directions to level the leaf. Repeat steps 6 and 7 to add the remaining leaf to the opposite side of the table.

PAINTING TIPS:

The leaves of this table look like an embroidered dresser scarf, just like grandma used to make. The easiest way to imitate embroidery stitches is to use paint pens, but that limits your color selection. Painting with a brush is easy if you start with a good brush. My favorite is a #8 sable round point.

Wet your brush and load it with paint. Twirl the brush to form a point at the tip. Draw the point smoothly along the line.

For the loops that form the petals and leaves, leave a tiny space between the starting and end points. You can even add a tiny perpendicular line to the main "stitch," at the apex of the curve, to further imitate a lazy daisy stitch.

To make perfectly round, raised dots that look like French knots, dip the end of the paintbrush handle into the paint and touch it to the surface. Reload with paint after one or two dots.

PORCH BALUSTER TABLE

Vintage balusters bring the ambience of an old-fashioned
front porch into the house.

1 Cut a plywood tabletop in proportion to suit the balusters (ours is 42 × 20" [105 × 50 cm]); cut trim molding to fit, mitering the ends. Paint or finish the top and molding to match or complement the balusters. Attach the molding to the table-top, using glue and finish nails. Cut four 4½ × 4½" (11 × 11 cm) blocks of ½" (12 mm) birch, and drill a 5/16" (8 mm) hole through the center of each. Install a T-nut in each block.

2 Attach a block 1" (2.5 cm) from the corner on each side; secure the blocks with glue and ¾" (19 mm) wood screws.

3 Gang the balusters and compare them. Plane or sand them as necessary until the ends are flush with one another. At the top of each baluster, drill a ⅛" (3 mm) pilot hole and install a furniture bolt. Install the baluster legs by screwing the bolts into the T-nuts. If necessary, add leveling feet to the bottoms of the balusters.

MATERIALS:
• PORCH BALUSTERS (4) • ¾" (19 MM) BIRCH PLYWOOD • OGEE MOLDING • WOOD GLUE • 4D FINISH NAILS • SCRAP OF ½" (12 MM) BIRCH • ¾" (19 MM) WOOD SCREWS (4) • T-NUTS (4) • FURNITURE BOLTS (4)

MIRRORED TRAY TABLE

Serve leisurely breakfasts or afternoon tea on this lovely tray table.

1 Remove the backing, glass, and all hanging hardware from the frame, then clean and lightly sand it. Center a handle on each end and mark the positions. Drill countersunk holes through the ends of the frame. Position the handles then insert and tighten the screws until the handles are stable. Fill the holes with wood filler and sand them lightly.

2 Measure the opening in the back of the frame and cut a piece of ¼" hardboard to fit. Place the hardboard on the frame and drill a countersunk pilot hole every 3 to 4" (76 to 100 mm). Drill a pilot hole near each corner as well as through the center of each candle cup.

3 Spray primer on the frame, backing, candle cups, and folding legs and let them dry. Add two coats of silver spray paint, allowing the paint to dry between coats. Working on one piece at a time, apply antiquing medium then wipe away the excess, using a clean, dry cloth. When the antiquing medium is dry, spray the pieces with sealer and let them dry. Position the mirror within the frame, add the backing, and screw the backing to the frame. Screw the candle cups to the corners of the backing. Rest the tray on the folding legs. (The candle cups will hold it in place.)

MATERIALS:

• SALVAGED FRAME, AT LEAST 12 × 24" (305 MM × 610 MM) • SALVAGED FOLDING LEGS OR LUGGAGE STAND • HANDLES (2) • LATEX WOOD FILLER • ¼" (6 MM) HARDBOARD • ¾" (19 MM) WOOD SCREWS • PRIMER • SILVER SPRAY PAINT • BLACK ANTIQUING MEDIUM • SEALER • MIRROR CUT TO FIT FRAME • WOOD CANDLE CUPS (4)

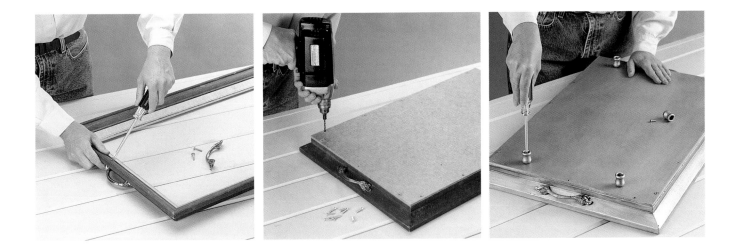

LOG OTTOMAN

Rest your feet or a snack tray on this simple ottoman.

1 Cut a 16 to 20" (40.64 to 50.8 cm) slice of a tree trunk. Hand plane the top until it's smooth and even. Set the log upside down on a level work surface, and use a carpenter's square to mark a consistent cutting line. Start this cut with a circular saw, following the line around the log; finish with a reciprocating saw or handsaw. Sand the top with a fine-grade sanding sponge. Remove any sawdust, dirt, or debris from the bark with a stiff-bristled brush, then apply two coats of varnish to the bark and cut surfaces. Let the varnish dry.

2 Drill pilot holes and attach three equally spaced casters to the bottom of the log.

MATERIALS:

• LARGE TREE TRUNK OR LOG • FINE-GRADE SANDING SPONGE

• WATER-BASED, SATIN-FINISH POLYURETHANE VARNISH

• CASTERS (3)

CHAIR TOPIARY

This conversation piece literally grows on you over time.

1 Shape chicken wire around the back and legs of a wooden or metal chair. Use wire cutters to trim the chicken wire, and florist's wire to join the sections. Cover the seat with 6 mil plastic, then form the chicken wire into a shallow basketlike shape over it.

2 Cover the chicken wire with damp moss. Cut 3" (7.5 cm) pieces of florist's wire and bend each in half; use these to hold the moss in place. Wrap fishing line around the arms and legs, and tie the moss in place. Mix moisture-retention crystals into potting soil, and fill the seat area. Plant baby's tears (Soleirolia soleirolii) in the seat area. Mist the topiary regularly and water it carefully. Make sure it gets plenty of light, but keep it out of direct sun.

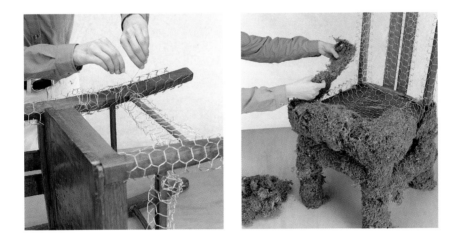

MATERIALS:

• CHAIR • CHICKEN WIRE • SHEET MOSS • FISHING LINE • FLORIST'S WIRE
• 6 MIL PLASTIC • POTTING SOIL • MOISTURE-RETENTION CRYSTALS
• TRAILING PLANT SUCH AS BABY'S TEARS

MOSAIC CHAIR

When life gives you broken dishes, make a mosaic!

1 *Loosen the bolts holding the chair bottom; remove the plywood and upholstery materials. Trace the outline of the chair frame onto the plywood.*

2 *If you're trying to preserve a center medallion, put masking tape across the back of the plate. Place the plate in a paper bag and tap it with a rubber mallet. Use tile nippers to refine the pieces. Glue the pieces to the plywood, within the outline of the frame.*

3 *Replace the plywood and tighten the bolts. Apply grout to the mosaic. Use a damp sponge to clean away the excess grout. Rinse the sponge frequently and keep wiping until all the grit has been removed. Several hours later, remove the grout film by polishing the mosaic with a dry cloth.*

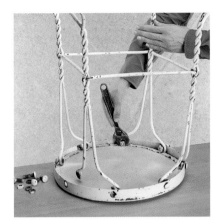

MATERIALS:
• ICE CREAM–PARLOR CHAIR • CHINA PLATES • SILICONE GLUE • GROUT

TWIG CHAIR

Create a woodsy garden effect with a twig chair accent.

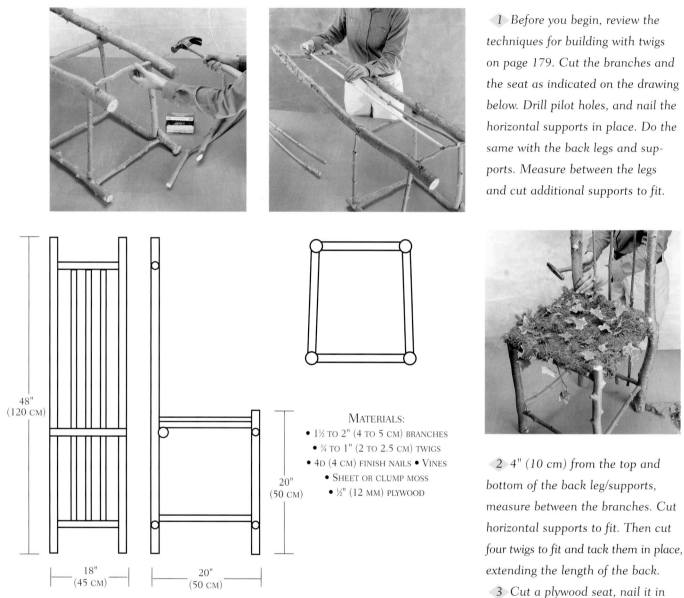

1 Before you begin, review the techniques for building with twigs on page 179. Cut the branches and the seat as indicated on the drawing below. Drill pilot holes, and nail the horizontal supports in place. Do the same with the back legs and supports. Measure between the legs and cut additional supports to fit.

48" (120 CM)

18" (45 CM)

20" (50 CM)

20" (50 CM)

MATERIALS:
- 1½ TO 2" (4 TO 5 CM) BRANCHES
- ¾ TO 1" (2 TO 2.5 CM) TWIGS
- 4D (4 CM) FINISH NAILS • VINES
- SHEET OR CLUMP MOSS
- ½" (12 MM) PLYWOOD

2 4" (10 cm) from the top and bottom of the back leg/supports, measure between the branches. Cut horizontal supports to fit. Then cut four twigs to fit and tack them in place, extending the length of the back.

3 Cut a plywood seat, nail it in place, and hot glue moss to cover it.

FIVE-BOARD BENCH

Place this classic bench in front of a sofa, at the foot of a bed, or in a hallway.

1 *Cut the parts as indicated on the list below. On each leg, mark the V and the notches as shown in the diagram on page 82. Use a jigsaw to shape the legs. Also, make a mark 2" (50 mm) from the top and 2½" (65 mm) from the end on each end of the side pieces. Connect the marks, then cut along that line to shape the corners of the side pieces.*

Part	Material	Length	Number
Side	1 × 6	42" (1070 mm)	2
Top	1 × 10	42" (1070 mm)	1
Legs	1 × 10	17" (430 mm)	2

MATERIALS:

- 8 FT. (2400 MM) 1 × 10 (19 × 254 MM) • 8 FT. 1 × 6 (12 × 140 MM)
- 1⅝" (42 MM) DRYWALL SCREWS • LATEX WOOD FILLER • WATER-BASED STAIN
- SATIN-FINISH POLYURETHANE SEALER • LATEX PAINT (2 COLORS)
- DECORATIVE HANDLES (2)

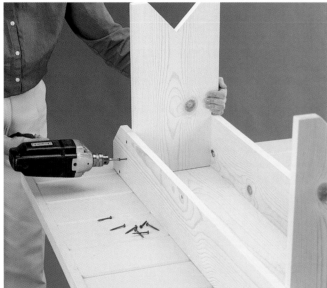

2 On a level work surface, set one side piece into the notches on the legs. At each leg, drill countersunk pilot holes and then secure each joint with three drywall screws.

3 Set the top into position, its edge flush with the face of the side piece. Drill three countersunk pilot holes across the top and a hole about every 9" (230 mm) along the edge. Attach the top to the legs and side with drywall screws.

4 Turn the assembly upside down, and add the remaining side. (The edge of the side will be flush with the face of the top.) Drill three countersunk pilot holes down the

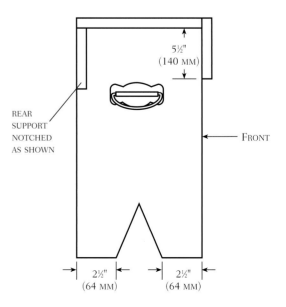

REAR
SUPPORT
NOTCHED
AS SHOWN

FRONT

5½"
(140 MM)

2½"
(64 MM)

2½"
(64 MM)

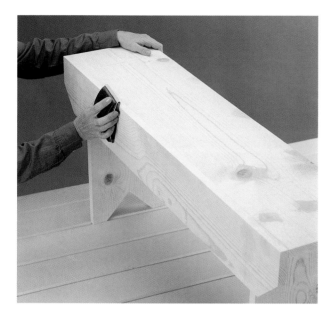

leg and a hole about every 9" along the edge. Drive drywall screws through the side and into the legs and top.

5 Fill all pilot holes with wood filler and allow them to dry. Lightly sand the entire bench, and remove the dust with a tack cloth. Apply a coat of stain to the bench and let it dry; add a coat of polyurethane sealer, and let that dry. Apply two coats of latex paint, a different color for each coat. Between coats, let the paint dry thoroughly, then lightly sand the bench, using fine-grit sandpaper. Wipe the bench with a tack cloth before applying the next

coat. To reveal the layers of color, sand the bench with medium-grit sandpaper, sanding more thoroughly in some areas than others to remove layers unevenly. Avoid sanding beyond the stain.

6 Center a handle 5½" (140 mm) from the top of each leg. Drill pilot holes and drive screws to attach the handles to the bench.

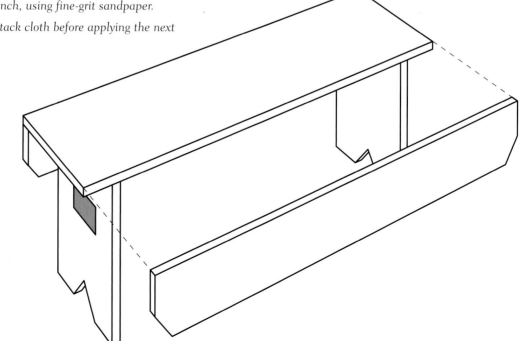

DOOR BENCH

The small, design-friendly frames of five-panel doors are
just right for this simple bench.

As you shop for doors, keep these tips in mind:
• doors should be roughly the same overall width, height, and thickness
• panel openings should be the same size
• stile and rail widths should be the same and milling details should be similar
Following our plans, each five-panel door yields three full-sized frame-and-panel units where the frame is full width on all four sides. Before you begin cutting, consider the placement of hinge or lockset mortises and other features of the doors.

Material	Part	No.	Dimensions
Three-panel frame	Back	1	28 × 49" (71.12 cm × 1.24 m)
Single-panel frames	Ends	2	17½ × 30" (44.45 × 76.2 cm)
Single-panel frames	Seat	2	17½ × 24½" (44.45 × 62.23 cm)
Single-panel frames	Kickboards	2	17½ × 24½" (44.45 × 62.23 cm)
2 × 4s	Frame supports	4	46" (1.17 m)
2 × 4s	Frame supports	4	14" (35.56 cm)
1 × 3s	Armrests	2	18½" (46.99 cm)

If it's not possible to match these dimensions from the doors you select, follow these guidelines: For the back, select a door that has a three-panel section that equals the width of two seat-panel frames, end-to-end. (If necessary, trim the stiles of the seat panels to match.) The middle stile sections, where the seat and kick panels meet, should combine to equal one full stile width. The width of the end panels should accommodate the depth of the seat panels plus the thickness of the back panel. (This can be adjusted by including some overhang on the front edge of the seat panels.)

MATERIALS:
FIVE-PANEL DOORS (3) • 8 FT. (2.44 M) 2 × 4S (5.08 × 10.16 CM) (2)
• 40" (1.02 M) 1 × 3 (2.54 × 7.62 CM)
• #10 2½" (6.35 CM) WOOD SCREWS • WOOD GLUE
• PRIMER • LATEX ENAMEL PAINT, BLACK

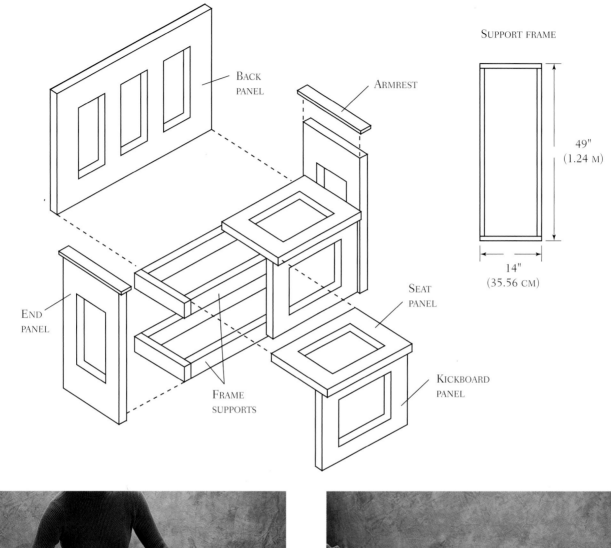

BACK
PANEL

ARMREST

SUPPORT FRAME

49"
(1.24 M)

14"
(35.56 CM)

END
PANEL

SEAT
PANEL

FRAME
SUPPORTS

KICKBOARD
PANEL

1 Remove any hardware remaining on the doors, then mark them, and use a straightedge and circular saw to cut parts as indicated on page 85. Compare the overall lengths of the back panel, seat and kick panel combinations. Adjust as necessary, then sand all edges. (If any of the frame joints come apart when you cut the doors, simply reglue the joints, clamp them together, and set them aside to dry.)

2 Following the diagram at left, lay out and assemble the 2 × 4 support frames. Use 2½" wood screws to secure the joints. Mark the seat and support frame positions on the end panels. Drill counterbored pilot holes and fasten end panels to the support frames, using glue and 2½" wood screws.

3 Position the back, drill pilot holes, and secure it, again using glue and wood screws. Next, install both seat pieces and both kickboards.

4 Position the 1 × 3 armrests over the end panels, with the edges flush along the insides of the panels, and the ends flush at the back of the bench, leaving a 1" (2.54 cm) overhang at the front. Attach the armrests with glue and wood screws.

5 Fill and sand the screw holes. Paint the bench with primer and two coats of black paint, allowing the paint to dry thoroughly between coats.

SIMPLE HEADBOARD

Build a simple headboard. Add sumptuous linens to make a restful place for body and soul.

1 Cut all parts listed below. Rout one edge of each piece of side and bottom trim, using a ⅜ × ½" (9.5 × 12.5 mm) piloted dado bit. On the front and back top trim pieces, make marks exactly 2" (50 mm) from each end. Starting and ending at these marks, rout the edge of each piece of top trim.

2 Lay out the top front trim with the dado facing up. Run a bead of wood glue along the dado, then fit the headboard base into position within the trim, precisely aligned with the 2" marks. Use pipe clamps to hold the trim in position against the base. Use a damp cloth to wipe away any excess glue, then let it dry.

3 Run a bead of glue along the dado on the back top trim, then clamp it in position on top of the base. Drill countersunk pilot holes and drive 1¼" drywall screws to secure the layers of trim. Again, wipe away any excess glue, and allow it to dry.

Part	Material	Size	Number
Base	Plywood	42 × 51" (1065 × 1295 mm)	1
Side Trim	1 × 3 poplar or clear pine	57⅜" (1455 mm)	4
Top Trim	1 × 3 poplar or clear pine	55" (1400 mm)	2
Bottom Trim	1 × 3 poplar or clear pine	52" (1320 mm)	2
Cap	1 × 3 poplar or clear pine	52" (1320 mm)	1

This headboard fits a full-size bed.

Note: When cutting trim pieces, especially front and back top trim, it's better to be slightly generous than short. If necessary, sand to fit.

MATERIALS:

4 × 8 FT. (1200 × 2400 MM) SHEET OF ¾" (19 MM) SOLID-CORE VENEER PLYWOOD • 1 × 3 (19 × 65 MM) POPLAR OR PINE (30 FT. [10 M]) • 1¼" (32 MM) DRYWALL SCREWS • WOOD GLUE • 4D (38 MM) FINISH NAILS • WOOD APPLIQUE • LATEX WOOD FILLER • PAINT • ANTIQUING GLAZE • VARNISH • FURNITURE SLIDES (4) • HOLLYWOOD BED FRAME

4 Repeat steps 2 and 3 with the back and front side trim, positioning the outside edges of the side trim flush with the ends of the top trim. At the bottom of the headboard, measure the opening between the side trim, then cut the front and back bottom trim to fit. Glue the front bottom trim in place and let it dry, then add the back bottom trim and screw the layers together as described in step 3.

5 Set the assembly right-side up and run a generous bead of glue along the top edge of the upper trim. Center the cap on this top edge, overlapping the edges by ½" (12 mm). Tack the cap in place with 4d finish nails and let the glue dry.

6 Position the wood applique and mark placement lines on the face of the headboard. Drill pilot holes in the applique, then spread wood glue on the back. Apply the applique, then tack it in place with 4d finish nails. Let the adhesive dry.

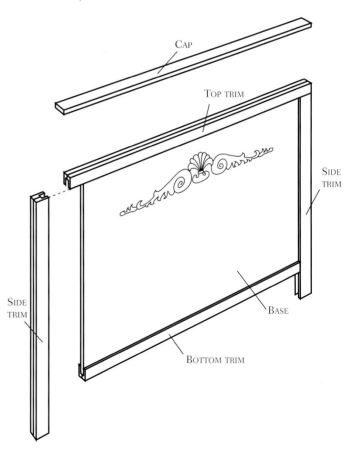

CAP

TOP TRIM

SIDE TRIM

SIDE TRIM

BASE

BOTTOM TRIM

7 Fill all holes with wood filler, lightly sand the entire headboard, then clean the surface with a tack cloth. Apply two coats of ivory paint, allowing the paint to dry between coats.

8 Working on one manageable area at a time, apply a coat of antiquing glaze. (We used Ralph Lauren's Aging Glaze in Tea Stain.) Brush with the grain of the wood. While the glaze is still wet, use a slightly damp rag to wipe off the excess, wiping perpendicular to the grain. Use a cotton swab to remove excess glaze in the crevices of the applique. (Don't remove too much—the crevices in most old pieces are discolored by trapped dust.)

9 When the glaze is dry, apply two coats of varnish and let it dry. Tack a furniture slide to the bottom of each leg. Mark and drill holes in each leg, then use bolts to attach a Hollywood bed frame to the headboard.

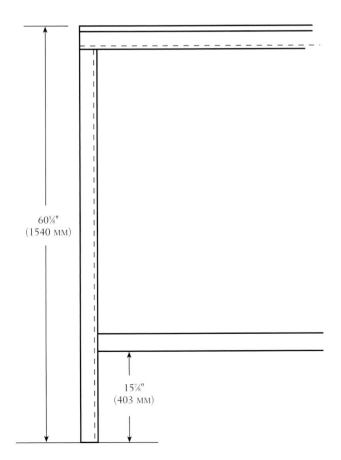

60⅜"
(1540 MM)

15⅞"
(403 MM)

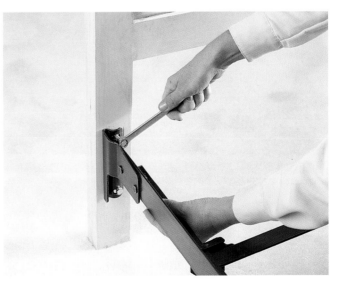

GARDEN WALL HEADBOARD

This headboard will give you the feeling of sleeping beneath a garden wall.

1 *Clamp two cedar 4 × 4s (10 × 10 cm) together and mark cutting lines for the dadoes as shown in the diagram on page 94. Set the cutting depth on a circular saw to exactly match the thickness of the 2 × 4 (5 × 10 cm) stringers. Between the lines marked for the dadoes, make cuts across the posts, one cut every ¼" (6 mm). Use a chisel to remove the waste material within the dadoes. Set the stringers into position, their ends flush with the outside edges of the posts*

and their faces flush with the faces of the posts. Secure the stringers with 2½" (6 cm) drywall screws.

2 *Cut the plywood base and backing. Mark the setting lines for the tile on the base. Screw the base to the stringers and countersink the screws. Turn the assembly over and set the backing in place above the first stringer; align its edges with the edges of the base. Secure the backing by driving screws into it through*

(continued on page 94)

MATERIALS:
- 4 × 4 (10 × 10 CM) CEDAR POSTS (2) • ¾" (19 MM) PLYWOOD (1 SHEET)
- 2 × 4S (5 × 10 CM) (2) • 2½" (6 CM) DRYWALL SCREWS • LATEX UNDERLAYMENT
- MASKING TAPE • LATEX PAINT • 2 × 2" (5 × 5 CM) CERAMIC TILE
- TILE ADHESIVE • GROUT • LATEX ADDITIVE • DECK POST CAPS (2, OPTIONAL)
- GROUT SEALER • BOLTS • SEMI-GLOSS POLYURETHANE • HOLLYWOOD BED FRAME

(continued from page 93)

the front of the base. Countersink the screws and fill the holes with latex underlayment. Mix paint into drywall compound at a ratio of 1:4. Mask off the tile area, including the top edge of the assembly. Using a drywall knife or 12" (30 cm) square-end trowel, spread the paint/wallboard compound mixture onto the unmasked portion of the base and backing, and then to the posts. Sweep across the compound, pressing down on one edge of the trowel or drywall knife to create a textured appearance. When the compound is completely dry, seal it with a coat of semi-gloss polyurethane.

3 Lay out the tile and plan its placement. If necessary, use a tile cutter and nippers to trim the tile to fit.

4 Working on 18 to 24" (45 to 60 cm) at a time,

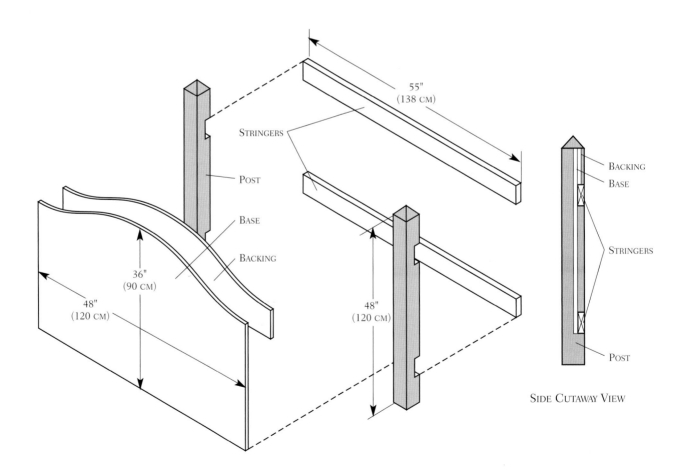

STRINGERS

POST

BASE

BACKING

55"
(138 CM)

36"
(90 CM)

48"
(120 CM)

48"
(120 CM)

BACKING
BASE

STRINGERS

POST

SIDE CUTAWAY VIEW

spread tile adhesive on the top of the unfinished plywood of the base and backing. Set the field tile flush with the edge of the base and then the edge tile flush with the face of the field tile. Press each tile firmly into the adhesive, twisting the tile slightly to settle it in place.

5 When the tile adhesive is dry, mix the grout and latex additive. Apply the grout, then wipe away the excess with a damp sponge. Rinse the sponge frequently and continue wiping until all the excess is removed. Let the grout dry for an hour, then polish the powdery film off of the tile. Allow the grout to cure as directed by the manufacturer before sealing it.

6 Mark and drill holes in the posts, then use bolts to attach a Hollywood bed frame to the headboard. Optional: Paint deck-post caps to complement the textured surface and add one to each post.

COPPER HEADBOARD

Simple combinations of copper pipe and fittings produce an interesting headboard that costs under $100 to construct.

1 *Following the diagram on page 98, cut all the rigid copper pieces to length. Mark the holes on the middle (¾" [19 mm]) and lower (1¼" [3 cm]) rails; centerpunch and drill ½" (12 mm) holes through only the first wall of each rail. On each upper post, mark the holes for the middle rail. Next, center-punch the hole locations and then drill a ¾" (19 mm) hole through only the first wall of each upper post.*

2 *Lay out the middle and lower rails, and fit the braces between them. If necessary, use a rotary tool to tailor the holes until the pieces fit securely. Make sure the braces extend as far as possible into the rails—they support and strengthen them. Next, construct each post by using a 1¼" (3 cm) tee to connect the upper and lower post pieces. Finally, connect the rail-and-brace assembly to the posts. Insert the middle rail into the hole on each post and the lower rail into the*

tee on each side. Make sure the middle rail extends as far as possible into the posts. Top each post with a 1¼ × ½" (30 × 12 mm) reducer and put a 1¼" (3 cm) end cap on the bottom of each.

3 *Cut a 6-ft. (1.8 m) piece of ½" (12 mm) flexible copper for the upper rail. At one end, form an arc with a 5" (12 cm) radius, and then insert the end of the arc into the reducer at the top of one of the posts. At the other end, shape an arc that brings the end of the rail down to meet the reducer fitting on the second post. Trim the ends so the legs of the arcs are of equal length and the rail sits level across the headboard.*

4 *Clean and flux the joints, then dry-fit the pieces on a level, flame-resistant sur-*

MATERIALS:

½" (12 MM) RIGID COPPER (12 FT. [3.6 M])

• ¾" (19 MM) RIGID COPPER (5 FT. [1.5 M])

• 1¼" (3 CM) RIGID COPPER (12 FT. [3.6 M])

• ½" (12 MM) FLEXIBLE COPPER (APPROX. 8 FT. [2.4 M])

• 1¼ × ½" (30 × 12 MM) COPPER REDUCERS (2)

• 1¼" (3 CM) COPPER END CAPS (2)

• 1¼" (3 CM) COPPER TEES

• ¼" (6 MM) COPPER TUBING (10-FT. [3 M] ROLL)

• HOLLYWOOD BED FRAME • NUTS AND BOLTS

• 12-GAUGE (2MM) WIRE

face. Solder the joints, working from the bottom of the head-board and alternating from side to side. Check from time to time to make sure the assembly remains square and flat. (For more information on soldering, see page 180.)

◆ *5 To form the scrollwork: Cut two 30" (75 cm) pieces of ¼" (6 mm) copper tubing. Flatten both ends of one piece of tubing. Use locking pliers to clamp one end of the tubing to the top edge of a one-gallon paint can. Wrap about 15" (38 cm) of the tubing around the paint can, then remove it and reclamp the end to a piece of 1½" (4 cm) PVC pipe. Rotate the pipe to curl about 4" (10 cm) of the copper around the pipe, not quite one full rotation. Clamp the opposite end of the tubing to the PVC pipe and curl another 4" (10 cm). Repeat with the second 30" (75 cm) piece of tubing, checking after each step to make sure it matches the first.*

◆ *6 Mark the center point of the upper and middle rails and set the first scroll between them. Unroll the tubing into a graceful curve that allows the large end of the scroll to align with the center point of the headboard and the small end to contact the middle rail about 6" (15 cm) from the post. Repeat*

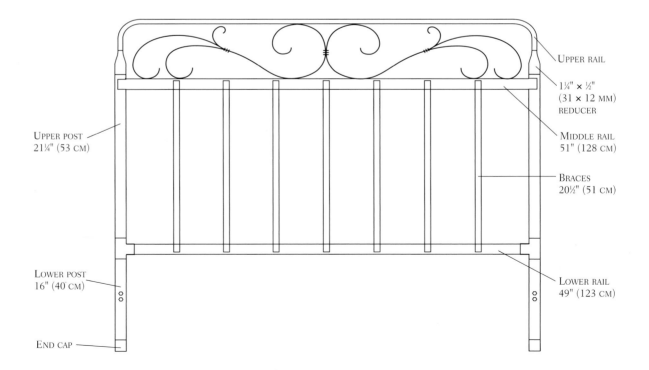

UPPER RAIL

1¼" × ½"
(31 × 12 MM)
REDUCER

MIDDLE RAIL
51" (128 CM)

UPPER POST
21¼" (53 CM)

BRACES
20½" (51 CM)

LOWER POST
16" (40 CM)

LOWER RAIL
49" (123 CM)

END CAP

this process to form the opposite scroll.

7 ▸ *Flatten both ends of two 12" (30 cm) and two 6" (15 cm) pieces of ¼" (6 mm) tubing. Curl one end of each 12" (30 cm) piece around the PVC pipe and unwind it to form a gentle curve that contacts the middle rail about 2" (5 cm) from the post and reaches to a point about 6" (15 cm) beyond the small end of the original scroll. Curl each 6" (15 cm) piece around the 1½" (4 cm) piece of PVC pipe, and unwind it to repeat the pattern of the small end of the original scroll. Set this piece in place to contact the original scroll just before the end of the 12" (30 cm) scroll described above. (It does not contact the upper rail.) Repeat this process to complete the scrollwork on the opposite side of the headboard.*

8 ▸ *Clean and flux the contact spots on the tubing and upper and middle rails. Solder the tubing into position. Wrap 12-gauge (2 mm) wire around the tubing, forming 1" (2.5 cm) coils that conceal the joints.*

9 ▸ *Drill holes through each post and use nuts and bolts to secure a Hollywood frame to the headboard.*

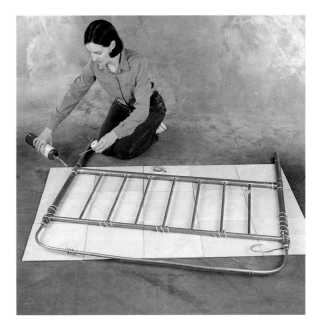

FISH HEADBOARD

A whole new—and pleasant—way to "sleep with the fishes."

1 Clamp two cedar 4 × 4 fence posts together and mark cutting lines for the dadoes as shown in the diagram on page 102. Set the cutting depth on a circular saw to exactly match the thickness of the 2 × 4 stringers. Between the lines marked for the dadoes, make cuts across the posts, one cut every ¼" (6.4 mm). Use a chisel to remove the waste material within the dadoes. Set the stringers into position, their ends flush with the outside edges of the posts and their faces flush with the faces of the posts. Secure the stringers with 2½" drywall screws. Thoroughly sand the entire assembly.

2 Cut the MDF base and backing, and rout the top edges of each with a roundover bit. Apply a coat of primer to both sides and all the edges of each piece, and let it dry. Screw the base to the stringers and countersink the screws. Turn the assembly over and set the backing in place above the first stringer; align it so the top extends ½" (12.7 mm) beyond the top of the base. Drive screws through the backing and into the base.

(continued on page 102)

MATERIALS:
• 48" (1.22 M) 4 × 4 (10.16 × 10.16 CM) CEDAR FENCE POSTS (2)
• ¾" (19.1 MM) MDF (ONE 4 × 8 FT. [1.22 × 2.44 M] SHEET) • 2 × 4S (5.08 × 10.16 CM) (2) • 2½" (6.35 CM) DRYWALL SCREWS • TACK CLOTH • LATEX PRIMER • STENCIL MEDIA • STENCIL ADHESIVE • MODELING COMPOUND • LATEX PAINT • SATIN-FINISH POLYURETHANE • HOLLYWOOD BED FRAME • 2" (5.08 CM) HEX-HEAD BOLTS

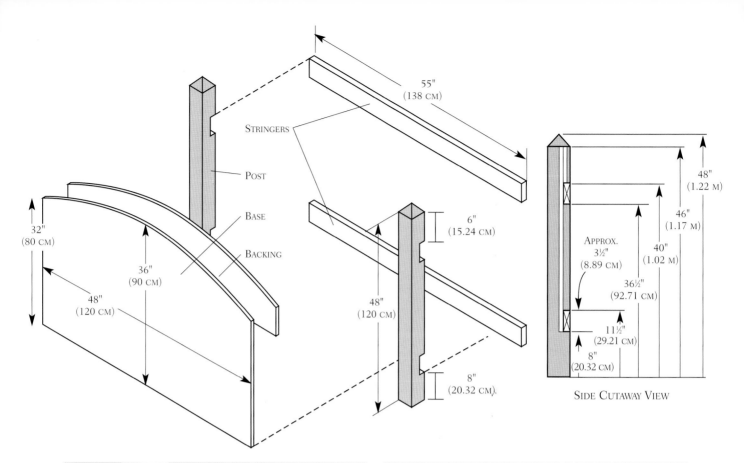

STRINGERS

POST

BASE

BACKING

55"
(138 CM)

6"
(15.24 CM)

32"
(80 CM)

36"
(90 CM)

48"
(120 CM)

48"
(120 CM)

8"
(20.32 CM)

48"
(1.22 M)

46"
(1.17 M)

40"
(1.02 M)

36½"
(92.71 CM)

APPROX.
3½"
(8.89 CM)

11½"
(29.21 CM)

8"
(20.32 CM)

SIDE CUTAWAY VIEW

(continued from page 101)

◆ 3 Photocopy and enlarge the pattern on page 185. Set a piece of glass over the pattern, then lay a piece of stencil media over the glass. Cut the stencil, using a stencil burner.

◆ 4 Mark the center of the headboard and make placement marks for the design. Spray the back of the stencil with stencil adhesive and secure it to the headboard. Spread a layer of modeling compound across the stencil, taking care to fill in all open areas. While the modeling compound is wet, remove the tape and peel off the stencil. Let the compound dry completely. Add layers until the design is approximately ³⁄₁₆" (4.8 mm) thick. Carefully clean the stencil between applications and make sure each layer is thoroughly dry before adding another. On the last coat, use the putty knife to texture the surface in much the same way you swirl frosting on a cake.

◆ 5 Paint the entire headboard with a base coat of soft yellow, and let it dry. Add a coat of soft green glaze. While the glaze is still slightly wet, wipe it with a damp sponge, removing glaze so that the base coat shows through in some areas. Pat the raised design with the sponge, leaving enough paint so that the design is shadowed and emphasized. Let the paint dry completely. (For additional information, see page 175.) Lightly sand selected areas to imitate wear patterns, then wipe away the sanding dust with a tack cloth. Dip an old toothbrush in dark green or black paint and pat it nearly dry on paper towels. Working in one small area at a time, scrape your fingernail across the toothbrush bristles to spatter paint across the headboard. Let the paint spatters dry completely, then seal the entire headboard with two coats of polyurethane.

◆ 6 Mark and drill holes in the posts, and then use bolts to attach a Hollywood bed frame to the headboard.

$\mathscr{L}$IGHTING

Good lighting is critical to any room, and appealing light fixtures are essential to good lighting. That's not news to most of us, but the idea of making lamps and chandeliers might be.

Don't worry. You really can do this. Read through the wiring techniques found on page 182—you'll find that wiring a lamp is neither difficult nor time consuming.

Once you discover how easy it is to make one, you'll begin seeing potential lamps all over the place. Go with it. The fact of the matter is, you can make a lamp out of almost anything. If you can make holes for the wires or attach the item to a base, you can make it into a lamp. All it takes is a little time, a little imagination, and a fair amount of confidence.

For the romantics among you (and for those who remain resistant to the idea of wiring), we've included projects that rely on candle power, such as the iron chandelier (page 116), the hanging lantern (page 124), and the gilded candlesticks (page 128).

These projects start with simple, readily available materials such as flat iron bars, twisted six-strand wire, and wood balusters. The materials may be simple, but the results, we assure you, are spectacular.

TEACUP LAMP

Stacked teacups make a delightful lamp for a bedside table.

1 Drill a ½" (12 mm) hole in the center of each cup and saucer. Support each piece in a bucket of sand; use a glass and tile bit and drill slowly. Stack the teacups and measure them. Purchase a threaded nipple that will accommodate the stack and leave about ½" (12 mm) at the top; purchase one 1" (2.5 cm) coupler for each inch of the nipple. (Allowing about 1" [2.5 cm] between cups, we used a 13" [33 cm] nipple and 13 couplers.) Slide a lock washer and a hex nut onto one end of the threaded nipple. Insert the nipple into the hole of the lamp base. Place a rubber washer over the nipple.

2 Set the first cup and saucer in place, add a rubber washer and a brass washer, then screw four brass couplers onto the threaded nipple. Add a brass washer and a rubber washer, the second cup, and a second set of washers; repeat to add the third cup. Screw on four more couplers, and top the assembly with a threaded brass washer, a harp, and another threaded brass washer.

3 Attach a socket cap to the nipple. Insert a lamp cord through the base and the nipple. Tie the split ends of the wire in an underwriter's knot, connect them to the lamp socket, and assemble the socket (see page 182). Add a lampshade and, if desired, a finial.

MATERIALS:

• CHINA CUPS AND SAUCERS (3 SETS) • THREADED NIPPLE
• LOCK WASHER (1) • HEX NUT (1) • 1" (2.5 CM) BRASS COUPLERS
(ONE FOR EACH INCH OF THREADED NIPPLE) • BRASS WASHERS (6)
• RUBBER WASHERS (6) • LAMP BASE • HARP • SOCKET CAP
• LAMP SOCKET • LAMPSHADE

TEAPOT LAMP

Brighten an occasional table or writing desk with a lamp made from a tea-for-one.

1 Center and drill a ½" (12 mm) hole in the cup and pot of a tea-for-one. (The one we used is by Tracy Porter.) Support each piece in a container of sand; use a rotary tool and a silicon carbide grinding stone. If the lid has a handle, use the rotary tool and a cut-off disc to cut a ⅝" (15 mm) opening in it. Finally, drill a ½" hole through the center of the lid.

2 Slide a lock washer and a hex nut onto one end of a threaded brass rod. Insert the rod into the hole of the lamp base and add a lock washer and hex nut below the base. Tighten the nuts against one another until the rod is stable. Put the rod through the hole in the cup and position the cup on the base. Squirt a bead of silicone caulk around the edges of the hole to make a buffer between the rod and the china. Add the teapot and put silicone around its hole. Thread a coupler and a second brass rod onto the first, then add the teapot's lid. Add silicone around the hole in the lid.

3 Top the brass rod with a threaded brass washer, a harp, another threaded brass washer, and a socket cap. Insert a lamp cord through the base and up through the top. Tie the split ends of the wire in an underwriter's knot, connect them to the lamp socket, and assemble the socket (see page 182). Add a lampshade and, if desired, a finial.

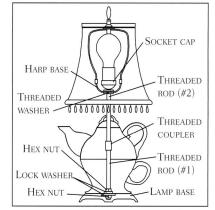

SOCKET CAP

HARP BASE

THREADED WASHER

THREADED ROD (#2)

HEX NUT

LOCK WASHER

HEX NUT

THREADED COUPLER

THREADED ROD (#1)

LAMP BASE

MATERIALS:

• TEA-FOR-ONE • BRASS LAMP BASE • LOCK WASHERS (2)
• HEX NUTS (2) • 5" (130 MM) THREADED BRASS LAMP ROD (2)
• SILICONE CAULK • 1" (25 MM) BRASS COUPLER • THREADED BRASS
WASHERS (2) • HARP • SOCKET CAP • LAMP SOCKET
• LAMP CORD • LAMPSHADE

BIRDCAGE LAMP

A birdcage with an interesting shape and intricate details makes a particularly good choice for this project.

1 If the cage doesn't have feet, add small blocks or dowels to act as a base. If necessary, drill a hole through the top of the birdcage. (We had to first cut off a knurl.) Insert a brass pipe threaded on each end. Above the wires on the bottom of the cage, add a threaded nut and a fender washer; below the wires add a fender washer, a lock nut, and a threaded nut. Tighten the threaded nuts to hold the pipe in place.

2 Add a threaded knurl nut and then a harp to the top of the brass pipe; attach the socket cap. Pull the lamp cord through the brass pipe and into the socket cap. Tie the split ends of the wire in an underwriter's knot, connect them to the lamp socket, and assemble the socket (see page 182). Add a lampshade and, if you like, a finial.

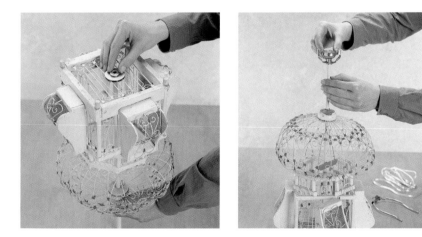

MATERIALS:
• BIRDCAGE • THREADED NUTS (2) • FENDER WASHERS (2) • LOCK NUT
• THREADED KNURL NUT • THREADED BRASS PIPE • SOCKET CAP • SOCKET
• LAMP CORD • LAMPSHADE

BIRCH LOG LAMP

Light up a room with this perfectly natural floor lamp.

1 *For the base, cut a 15" (38.1 cm) circle of plywood, and drill a ⅜" (9.5 mm) hole in the center. Route the edge with an ogee bit, if desired. Paint the base and toy wheels with acrylic paint. Put a flat washer, lock washer, and a hex nut onto one end of the threaded nipple. Insert the nipple up through the center of the base, and tighten the hex nut to set the lock washer.*

2 *Cut four 10"-long (25.4 cm) birch logs. Use a ½" (12.7 mm) auger bit to drill a hole through the center of each log. Slide two toy wheels onto the nipple, and*

add a log. Continue alternating between sets of toy wheels and logs, ending with two toy wheels. Top the wheels with a brass cap, then thread the brass couplers onto the nipple. Approximately ½" (12.7 mm) of the nipple should extend beyond the last coupler.

3 *Top the nipple with a threaded brass washer and then a harp; attach a socket cap. Pull the lamp cord through the nipple and into the socket cap. Tie the split ends of the wire in an underwriter's knot, connect them to the lamp socket, and assemble the socket (see page 182). Add a lamp shade and, if you like, a finial.*

MATERIALS:

• ¾" (19.1 MM) BIRCH PLYWOOD • 2" (5.08 CM) WOODEN TOY WHEELS (12) • DARK BROWN ACRYLIC PAINT
• ¾" (19.1 MM) DRYWALL SCREWS • 52" (132.08 CM) THREADED NIPPLE • 2 TO 2½"-DIAMETER (5.08 TO 6.35 CM) BIRCH BRANCHES
• FLAT WASHER (1) • LOCK WASHER (1) • HEX NUT (1) • BRASS CAP (1) • 1" (2.54 CM) BRASS COUPLERS (3) • THREADED BRASS
WASHER (1) • HARP • SOCKET CAP • LAMP SOCKET • LAMP CORD • LAMP SHADE

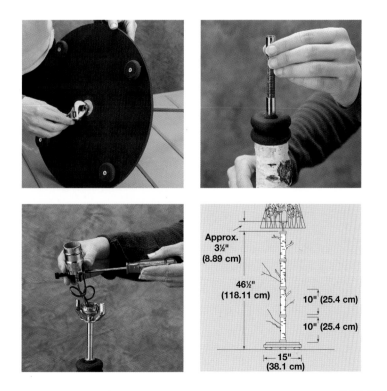

Approx.
3½"
(8.89 cm)

46½"
(118.11 cm)

10" (25.4 cm)

10" (25.4 cm)

15"
(38.1 cm)

PINECONE LAMP

Pinecones, enduring symbols of nature, make lovely lamps for rustic settings.

1 Snip out the top ½" (12.7 mm) of the center of the pinecone. Wrap the pinecone in bubble wrap, and clamp it in a workbench or vise with the base of the pinecone facing up. Using a 12"-long (30.48 cm), ½" (12.7 mm) auger bit, drill a hole all the way through the pinecone.

2 Slide a lock washer and a hex nut onto one end of the threaded brass pipe. Insert the pipe up through the center of the lamp base, and add a threaded brass washer. Tighten the nut and the washer until the pipe is steady within the base.

3 Insert the brass pipe into the hole in the pinecone and gently slide the pinecone down to the base. Top the pipe with a threaded brass washer and then a harp; attach a socket cap. Pull the lamp cord through the nipple and into the socket cap. Tie the split ends of the wire in an underwriter's knot, connect them to the lamp socket, and assemble the socket (see page 182). Add a lamp shade and, if you like, a finial.

Note: The height of the threaded brass pipe should be in proportion to the size of the pinecone. This pinecone is approximately 8" (20.32 cm) tall, so we used an 11" (27.94 cm) threaded brass pipe.

MATERIALS:

- LARGE PINECONE • BUBBLE WRAP • LAMP BASE • HEX NUT
- LOCK WASHER • FLAT METAL WASHER
- THREADED BRASS WASHERS (2) • BRASS PIPE THREADED AT EACH END
- HARP • SOCKET CAP • LAMP SOCKET
- LAMP CORD • LAMP SHADE

IRON CHANDELIER

Welcome family and friends to the table with the warm glow of this chandelier.

1 Use a reciprocating saw with a metal-cutting blade to cut the flat iron into five 24" (60.96 cm) pieces and five 16" (40.64 cm) pieces. (Wear heavy gloves and safety glasses.) Mark each 24" piece, 9½" (24.13 cm) from one end. Select bending forms: Any heavy-duty, round objects with solid edges will work. (We used a 10" automobile flywheel, a 6" toilet

flange, a 2" pipe flange, and a piece of 1" threaded pipe.) Attach the forms to 2 × 6 (5.08 × 15.24 cm) scraps that can be clamped into a workbench or bench vise.

2 For each 16" piece, clamp the iron to the 10" form, and shape the entire length of the piece. Lightly tap the iron with a hammer, if necessary, to get it to conform. Remove the iron

MATERIALS:

- 10" (25.4 CM), 6" (15.24 CM), 2" (5.08 CM), AND 1" (2.54 CM) BENDING FORMS
- 3⅛ × ¾ × 72" (7.9 CM × 19.1 MM × 1.83 M) FLAT IRON BARS • HEAVY GLOVES
- SAFETY GLASSES • 2" (5.08 CM) THREADED BLACK PIPE COUPLERS (2)
- ½" (12.7 MM) × 10-32 PANHEAD MACHINE SCREWS AND NUTS (15 EACH)
- 2" (5.08 CM) WOODEN TOY WHEELS (4) • 2" (5.08 CM) THREADED NIPPLE
- 2½" (6.35 CM) THREADED NIPPLE • LOCK WASHERS (4)
- THREADED BRASS WASHERS (4) • THREADED BRASS CAPS • FINIAL
- ¾" (19.1 MM) × 10-32 PANHEAD MACHINE SCREWS AND NUTS (5)
- 2½" (6.35 CM) UNFINISHED STEEL BOBESCHES (5)
- BLACK DECOR CHAIN (APPROX. 4 FT. [1.22 M])

from the 10" form, reclamp one end to the 1" form, and shape that end into a tight curve. Repeat at the opposite end. For each 24" piece, clamp the marked end to the 6" bending form; wrap the iron around the form, shaping it just past the mark. Next, clamp that same end to the 2" form, and wrap the iron almost all the way around the form. Unwrap the large curve slightly, refining the scroll into a pleasing shape. To curve the other end

in the opposite direction, turn the piece over and clamp the opposite end to the 2" form; wrap the iron almost all the way around.

◆ 3 Set a straightedge on a large piece of paper. Lay out one 16" section and one 24" section along the straightedge, and adjust them until they form a pleasing shape. Mark the contact points onto the iron itself, then mark the apex of the large curve on the 24" piece. At each mark, punch and drill a ³⁄₁₆" (4.8 mm) hole. (See Sidebar for information on drilling iron.) Assemble the arm, joining the pieces with ½" machine screws and nuts. Trace the outline onto the paper; use this pattern to arrange and assemble the remaining arms.

◆ 4 Draw a centerline around the outside of each coupler. Using a square, mark five equidistant points around each coupler, along the centerline. Punch and drill a ³⁄₁₆" hole at each marked point. Attach the arms to the couplers, again using ½" machine screws and nuts. Attach the bobesches to the arms, using ¾" machine screws and nuts.

◆ 5 Enlarge the center holes in the wooden toy wheels, using a ²⁵⁄₆₄" (9.9 mm) bit. Slide a toy wheel onto the 2" threaded nipple, add a lock washer and a threaded washer, then tighten the threaded washer. Set this assembly inside the lower coupler, resting the toy wheel on the screws and nuts at the center. From beneath the coupler, slide a toy wheel onto the nipple; add a lock washer and a threaded washer, tightening the threaded washer as much as possible. Next, slide a toy wheel onto the 2½" threaded nipple; add a lock washer and a threaded washer and use a pair of pliers to tighten the threaded washer. Add the threaded

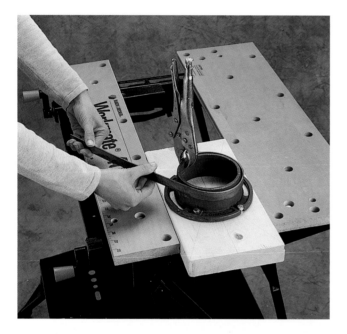

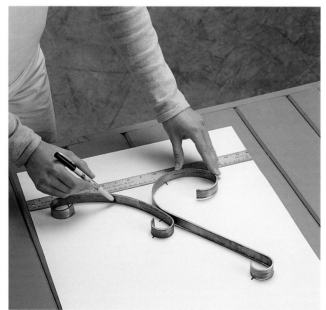

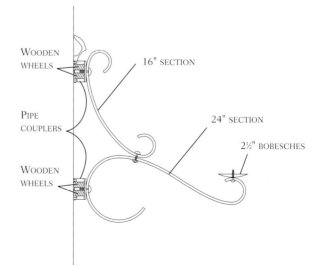

WOODEN WHEELS

16" SECTION

PIPE COUPLERS

24" SECTION

2½" BOBESCHES

WOODEN WHEELS

cap and tighten it by hand. Set this assembly inside the upper coupler, add a toy wheel, a lock washer, and a threaded brass washer. Use a pair of pliers to tighten the threaded washer. Top the stem with a threaded brass washer and a finial. Paint the entire chandelier and let it dry. (We used Metal Effects' iron paint and then added a rust activator.) Clip the chain into the finial, and it's ready to hang.

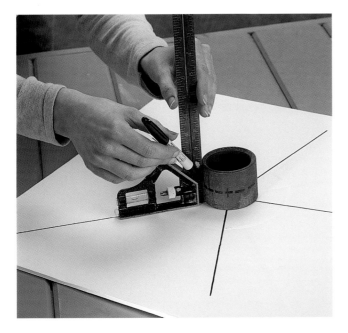

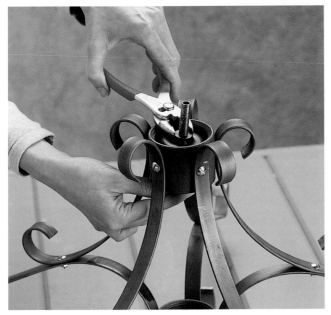

WORKING WITH IRON

When bending strips of cold rolled metal around forms, apply pressure at the first point where the metal meets the form (as shown below). Continue applying pressure in a fluid motion as you work around the form.

The keys to drilling holes in metal are:
• Use high-speed, carbon steel or tempered steel bits.
• Mark the starting point with a centerpunch.
• Keep the tip of the bit well oiled as you drill. A #10 oil, such as sewing machine oil, is best, but any light-weight oil will work.

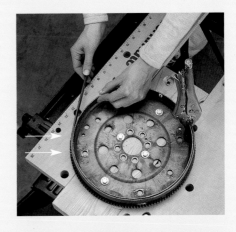

REFURBISHED CHANDELIER

Chandeliers are not just for dining areas anymore! Let them sparkle in unexpected places.

1   *Remove the light bulbs and sleeves from the sockets of the chandelier. Drill a hole at the front, back, and each side of each candle cup. Mark equally spaced holes around the perimeter of the rosette, each hole corresponding to an arm of the chandelier. If necessary, use a flat file or a rotary tool to polish away any rough edges on the holes.*

2   *Tape off the sockets, and rough up the chandelier's surface with coarse steel wool. Spray paint the entire chan-delier with two coats of base coat and let it dry. Holding the can within 8" (200 mm) of the surface, spray a moder-ately heavy layer of top coat onto the entire chandelier. (We used Plasti-kote's Cracklin' Gold base coat and Cream top coat. Read and follow manufacturer's directions for the product you select.) When the paint is dry, remove the masking tape from the sockets.*

MATERIALS:
- SALVAGED CHANDELIER • MASKING TAPE
- CRACKLE-FINISH SPRAY PAINT BASE COAT AND TOP COAT
- CRYSTAL PENDANTS • STRANDS OF PRISM BEADS
- DECORATIVE LAMPSHADES

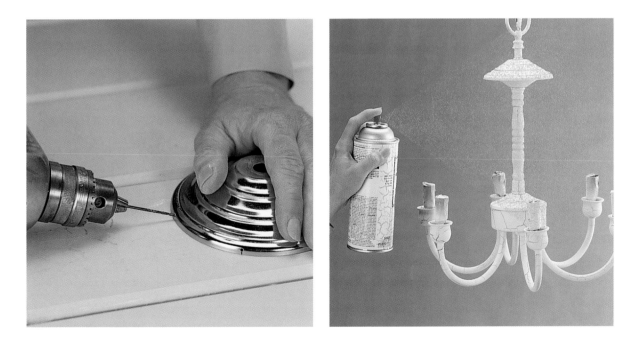

3 *Attach a strand of prism beads to a hole in the rosette and to the back of the corresponding candle cup. Experiment to find a length that allows the strand to droop gracefully. Cut additional strands of the same length, and attach one to each remaining set of holes.*

4 *Attach a strand of beads to the side of one candle cup and loop it toward the adjoining candle cup. Again, experiment to find a graceful length. Cut additional strands of the same length, and attach them between the arms.*

5 *Hang a crystal pendant from the hole in the front of each candle cup. Replace the sleeves and light bulbs, and add lampshades.*

Note: You can purchase inexpensive chandeliers from home centers, garage sales, and flea markets. We rescued this one from the center of a Tiffany-style fixture that had been discarded. We found the prisms and much more online at Chandelierparts.com.

MAKING DECORATIVE LAMPSHADES

You can find a wide variety of decorative lampshades for chandeliers these days,
but it may be less expensive and more fun to create your own.

For each, you'll need a self-adhesive lampshade, fabric, and decorative trim. Check the label on the lampshades for yardage requirements.

The paper protector on a self-adhesive shade also acts as a pattern. Peel the protector from the shade, and trace it onto your fabric, adding 1" (25 mm) all around for the seam allowance.

Next, cut out the fabric and place the wrong side on the shade, with the seam allowances extending past the top, bottom, and seam. Press the fabric onto the shade, and

smooth it from side to side and top to bottom to eliminate ripples or wrinkles. Trim the seams to ⅜" (10 mm), and use white glue to secure the overlapping seam.

Clip the top edge of the fabric every ½" (12 mm), then roll the seam allowance snugly over the wire edge and hot glue it to the inside of the shade. Roll the seam allowance snugly over the bottom edge and glue it to the inside of the shade as well.

Starting and stopping at the seam and gluing about 2" (50 mm) at a time, glue decorative trim to the edge of the shade.

HANGING LANTERN

Untwist six-strand copper wire and shape it into an ingenious
hanging loop for a garden lantern.

*1 Cut an 18" (45 cm) piece of ½" (12 mm) flexible
copper tubing and a 6-ft. (1.8 m) piece of ½" (12 mm)
rigid copper pipe. Form the flexible copper into a
curlicue as shown; solder an end cap onto one end and a
coupler onto the other. Solder the coupler to the copper
pipe, using an elbow, to form a hook. Plant the complet-
ed hook in the soil of a large potted plant.*

*2 Untwist the first 10" (25 cm) of a 24" (60 cm) piece
of twisted copper wire. Shape the individual strands
around a round 6" (15 cm) chandelier globe; use one
strand to band a pigtail at the bottom of the globe. Curl
the tails around a dowel, then bend them into a pleasing
arrangement. Wrap a piece of 16-gauge (1.5 mm) copper
wire around the lip of the globe to cradle it within the
wires. Form a loop at the opposite end of the twisted
wire; untwist and shape the first 4 or 5" (10 or 13 cm) of
each strand. Add sand and a votive candle, then hang
the lantern from the hook.*

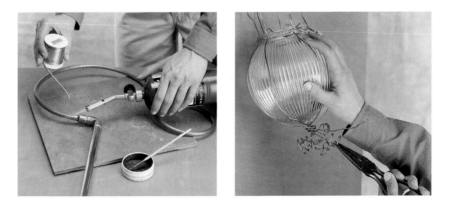

MATERIALS:
- ½" (12MM) FLEXIBLE COPPER TUBING • ½" (12 MM) COPPER PIPE
- ½" (12 MM) COPPER END CAP (1) • ½" (12 MM) COPPER COUPLER
- ½" (12 MM) COPPER ELBOW • 16-GAUGE (1.5 MM) COPPER WIRE • FINE SAND
- 6-STRAND TWISTED COPPER WIRE (2 FT. [60 CM]) • VOTIVE CANDLE • CHANDELIER GLOBE

CLOCHE LANTERN

The handblown glass and graceful shape of a garden cloche is
enhanced by candlelight.

*1 Measure the circumference of the cloche to determine
how big the hoops need to be. Flatten one end of a piece
of flexible copper tubing, clamp it onto a garden pail, and
shape it into a hoop. Mark and cut the tubing at the junc-
tion, then flare and solder the ends. Centerpunch three
equidistant points on the hoop, then drill a ⅜" (9 mm)
hole at each point. Repeat to form two more identical
hoops.*

*2 Cut three legs in a length appropriate for your cloche
(ours are 15" [38 cm]). For each, flatten one end and
clamp it to a 1" (2.5 cm) socket; hold the tubing firmly
and ratchet the wrench to coil the tubing. At the second
turn of the coil, bend the tubing at an angle to match the
shape of the cloche. (If you don't have a socket set, wrap
the tubing around a 1" [2.5 cm] dowel.) Cut nine 12" (30
cm) pieces of 12-gauge (2 mm) copper wire and wrap
each around a piece of ¼" (6 mm) tubing to form nine
1"-long (2.5 cm) coils.*

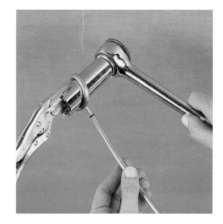

*3 Insert one leg into each hole in the first hoop; thread
one of the wire coils onto each leg. Repeat with the second and third hoops. Clean and flux the joints; set the
frame upside down and solder, working from the base of
the frame up toward the legs. Before you solder the foot
coils, adjust them to make sure the frame will sit level.*

MATERIALS:
- CLOCHE • ¼" (6 MM) FLEXIBLE COPPER TUBING
- GARDEN PAIL • 12-GAUGE (2 MM) COPPER WIRE

GILDED CANDLESTICKS

A perfect example of trash to treasure: Discarded balusters or bedposts become candlesticks.

1 *Cut the baluster or bedpost into two equal segments. In deciding where to cut, consider scale and proportion, and remember that the bottom of the finished candlestick needs to be heavier than the top. Drill a 1" (25 mm) hole in the center of the top of each candlestick, then lightly sand the surfaces.*

2 *Apply a base coat to each candlestick and let it dry. (We used Delta's Renaissance Foil Easy Crackle System.) Coat each candlestick with a coat of adhesive, and let it dry. Add a second coat of adhesive in an opposite or cross-wise direction. Let the adhesive dry for about an hour, or until it's clear and tacky. Lay a small piece of foil leaf onto an area, shiny side up, and burnish it with your finger or a smooth rubber tool. Push the foil firmly into hard-to-reach areas. Peel the foil away from its base and continue adding pieces of leaf, overlapping as necessary. To avoid creases and wrinkles, it's best to use small pieces on the curves and turned areas. Let the candlesticks dry for at least one hour.*

3 *Apply a heavy coat of crackle medium, using a soft-bristle brush. Let the crackle medium dry for twenty four hours; cracks will develop in the first hour or so. Spray a coat of sealer on each candlestick and let it dry. Apply a coat of antiquing glaze, and remove as much as desired, using a clean, soft cloth.*

MATERIALS:
- SALVAGED BALUSTER OR BEDPOST • BASE COAT • ADHESIVE
- GOLD OR SILVER FOIL • CRACKLE MEDIUM • SEALER
- ANTIQUING GLAZE

ACCESSORIES

By their very nature, accessories are small, interesting pieces that bring color, charm, and spirit to a room. These fun, easy-to-finish projects make wonderful accents for your own home, but they also make unique, thoughtful gifts for friends and family.

The projects in this chapter offer plenty of opportunities to let your creativity run wild. Start with wood balusters and newel posts in your favorite shapes and sizes. Build a basic clock (page 136), then embellish it any way you like. Or, twist aluminum pipe or silver solder to support your own collection of small vases or bottles (page 146).

Fun is the key ingredient in all these projects. Whether you're piping molding compound onto a picture frame or trimming a shrub into a fanciful spiral, you're sure to get a smile out of the process as well as the final product.

RUST-PAINTED MIRROR

Combine simple materials into a mirror that's a clear reflection of your good taste.

⬧ *1 Cut a 30 × 42" (76.2 cm × 1.07 m) piece of ½" MDF. Mark a 20 × 32" (50.8 × 81.28 cm) rectangle in the center, then drill a ¼" (6.4 mm) hole at each corner. Slip the blade of a jigsaw into a hole and cut out the rectangle, leaving a 5" (12.7 cm) frame. Cut two 29 × 41" (73.66 cm × 1.04 m) pieces of ¼" plywood. Cut a 22 × 36" rectangle out of the center of one of the plywood rectangles.*

⬧ *2 Cover one side of the MDF with wallpaper; carefully miter the paper around the inside and outside edges of the frame. Prime and paint the wallpaper. (We used primer, iron paint, and rust activator by Metal Effects.)*

⬧ *3 Run a zigzag bead of glue around the edges of one side of the plywood frame. Center the plywood frame on the back of the MDF frame. Set the mirror into the plywood frame so that its weight rests on the frame's edges. Top this assembly with the final plywood rectangle, and secure the layers with drywall screws placed every 4" (10.16 cm) around the perimeter. Apply a coat of polyurethane to the entire assembly and let it dry. Add the hanging hardware and wire.*

MATERIALS:

- ½" (12.7 MM) MDF • ¼" (6.4 MM) PLYWOOD
- PAINTABLE, TEXTURED WALLPAPER • LATEX PAINT
- MATTE-FINISH POLYURETHANE SPRAY • 22 × 36" (55.88 × 91.44 CM)
- MIRROR • POLYURETHANE GLUE • 1" (2.54 CM) DRYWALL SCREWS
- HANGING HARDWARE AND PICTURE WIRE

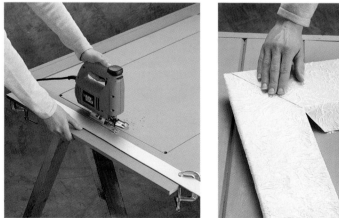

CHECKERBOARD

Keep this framed checkerboard hanging around—it's always ready for a quick game.

1 Cut a 20 × 20" (50.8 × 50.8 cm) square of MDF for the base. For the frame, rip 2½"-wide (6.35 cm) strips of plywood; cut the plywood strips and the crown molding into four 24" (60.96 cm) sections each. Using the base as a guide, cut the plywood strips to fit, mitering the ends at 45°. Clamp the strips in place and label them for placement.

2 Using the board and frame as a guide, cut the inner crown molding to fit, mitering the ends at 45°. Label these pieces for placement as well.

3 Seal all the pieces with pigmented shellac, and let them dry. Set the base on a level surface, on top of ¼" (6.4 mm) spacers. Reassemble the plywood pieces as marked, drill pilot holes, and nail the plywood to the base. Spread glue on the backs of the crown molding pieces, reassemble them as marked, and clamp them in place. Drill pilot holes, and nail the crown molding to the base.

4 Apply a coat of red paint to the entire assembly, and let it dry. Apply antiquing glaze to the frame and molding, and let it stand for about five minutes. Use the stippling brush to remove some of the glaze from the frame, then let it dry for at least an hour. Apply antiquing glaze to the board and immediately wipe it away with a cotton rag. Let the board dry overnight.

5 Following the directions on page 174, create a stencil for the checkerboard. Using the stencil, antiquing glaze, and a stencil brush, lightly paint the first set of squares. When the glaze is dry, turn the stencil 180° and paint the remaining squares. Let the board dry overnight. Cut 24" (60.96 cm) lengths of ruling tape, and apply them to the board as indicated on the pattern.

MATERIALS:

• ¾" (19.1 MM) MDF • ⅜" (9.5 MM) SOLID-CORE PLYWOOD
• CROWN MOLDING (8 FT. [2.44 M])
• PIGMENTED SHELLAC • ¼" PLYWOOD SCRAPS FOR SPACERS
• 6D FINISH NAILS • WOOD GLUE • LATEX PAINT (RED)
• BLACK ANTIQUING GLAZE • STIPPLING BRUSH
• TAGBOARD • ⅛" (3.2MM) BLACK RULING TAPE

CLOCKS

Cover a mantel or shelf with graceful clocks.

Spindle Clocks

MATERIALS:

- DECK OR STAIR BALUSTER OR NEWEL POST • WOOD GLUE
- DOWEL PINS • SPACKLE • CLOCK MOVEMENT OR SALVAGED
WATCH FACE • LATEX PAINT OR MATERIALS FOR SPECIALTY FINISHES
- RUBBER O-RING • BRASS COAT HOOKS (OPTIONAL)

1 *Study the baluster or post you've chosen and decide where to cut it and which portions to use to produce a well-balanced shape. Mark cutting lines and cut the spindle apart. On each section to be joined, mark a centerpoint and drill a hole for a dowel pin. Spread wood glue on the mating surfaces, and use dowel pins to connect the sections. Fill any gaps with spackle, then sand the finished spindle.*

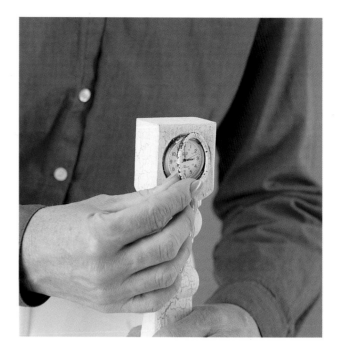

2 Measure the watch face, and decide where to position it. Mark a centerpoint, then use a spade bit to drill an appropriate hole. Cut a base scaled to suit the baluster or post, drill a hole in the center of each, and join them with glue and dowel pins. Optional: Mark three equidistant points around the base, then attach one brass coat hook at each mark.

3 Paint the spindle or give it a decorative finish, such as metallic leaf. (For the baluster clocks, we used an undercoat of taupe, crackle medium, and then ivory paint for a top coat. For the newel post clock, we used a yellow base coat topped with a pearl yellow glaze.) If you're using a watch face, as shown here, paint an O-ring and use it as a retaining ring to hold the watch face in place.

Mantel Clock

MATERIALS:

• 2" (50 MM) RIGID FOAM INSULATION • VENEER PLYWOOD
• CONSTRUCTION ADHESIVE • ½" (12 MM) MDF • DECORATIVE CORNER
CAPS • WOOD APPLIQUE • ⅛" (4 MM) WOOD DOWEL • WOOD GLUE •
WOODEN CANDLE CUPS • WOOD FILLER • PRIMER • LATEX PAINT
OR SPECIALTY FINISH • 1-GALLON (3.8 L) PAINT CAN • 3" (75 MM)
CLOCK MOVEMENT

1 Cut two blocks of rigid foam, one 5¾ × 2" (145 × 50 mm), and one 5¼ × 5¾" (135 × 145 mm). Trace the arc from a 1-gallon paint can onto the 5¾ × 2" block and use a coping saw to cut out the bonnet.

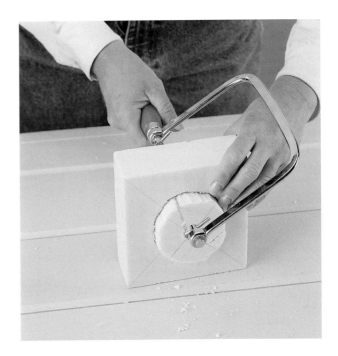

2 Use a protractor to scribe a 3" (75 mm) circle at the center of the block. Disassemble the coping saw, insert the blade through the foam, then reassemble the saw and cut along the marked line to cut the opening for the clock movement.

3 Trace the clock front and back of the body and the bonnet onto veneer plywood, and use a razor knife to cut out the pieces. Cut a 3" hole at the center of the front piece. Apply the veneer pieces to the blocks, using construction adhesive, such as Liquid Nails. For the arch of the bonnet, use masking tape to guide the veneer and to hold the veneer in place until the adhesive dries.

4 Cut four pieces of decorative corner cap, each piece 5¼" (135 mm) long. Glue one of these corner caps to each corner of the clock body; until the glue dries, hold the pieces in place with several rubber bands.

5 Cut two 7¾ × 4⅛" (200 × 105 mm) pieces of ½" MDF and rout the edges of each with a Roman ogee bit. On the bottom of one of the pieces of MDF (the base), drill a ⅛" (4 mm) pilot hole at each corner. Center the clock body between the cap and base, and use construction adhesive

to secure them. Let the adhesive dry thoroughly, then center the bonnet on the MDF cap and glue it in place. Cut four pieces of ⅛" dowel, each piece ¾" (20 mm) long. Glue these dowels into the pilot holes, and then glue the candle-cup feet in place over them. Finally, center a candle cup at the top of the bonnet and glue it in place.

◆ 6 Glue a wood applique to the center of the bonnet. Apply wood filler to all gaps and let it dry. Lightly sand the clock, apply a coat of primer, and let it dry. Finish as desired. (We painted ours with Powder Blue Americana Satin paint by DecoArt.) Insert the clock movement.

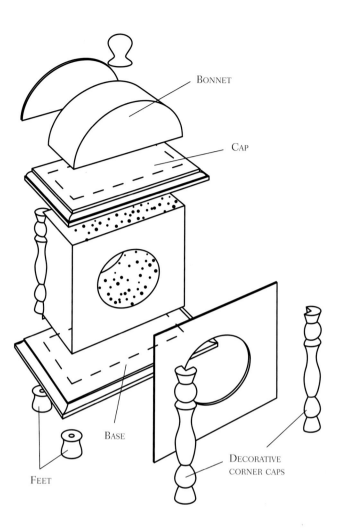

BONNET

CAP

BASE

FEET

DECORATIVE CORNER CAPS

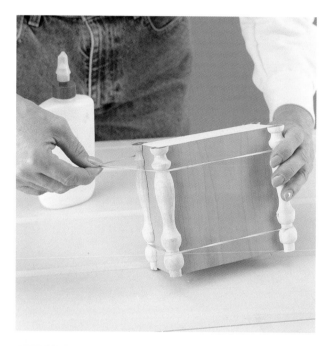

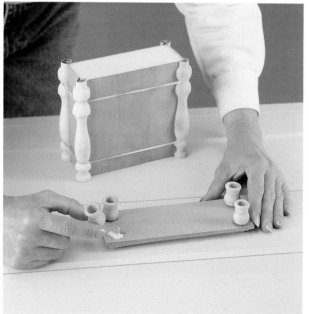

Half Moon
Mantel Clock

MATERIALS:

• 2" (50 MM) RIGID FOAM INSULATION • 1-GALLON (3.8 L) PAINT CAN
• PLYWOOD VENEER • ½" (12 MM) MDF • CONSTRUCTION ADHESIVE •
WOOD FILLER • WOOD CANDLE CUPS (5) • WOOD OR RESIN
APPLIQUES • PRIMER • PAINT • 3" (75 MM) CLOCK MOVEMENT

1 *Cut a 6¾ × 3⅜" (170 × 85 mm) block of rigid foam. Center the arc of a 1-gallon paint can on the block, and lightly scribe its shape into the foam.*

2 *Center the clock movement on the foam body and trace its shape. Cut out the marked circle (see step 2 on page 139). Trace the front and back of the foam block onto plywood veneer; draw a 2¹⁄₁₆ × 10¼" (52 × 260 mm) rectangle as well. Cut out the veneer; cut out a 3" (76 mm) hole centered in the front piece. Glue the veneer to the front, back, and top with construction adhesive. Hold the top in place with masking tape until the adhesive is dry. Cut an 8⅜ × 3½" (215 × 90 mm) piece of MDF for the base and rout the edges with a Roman ogee bit. Remove the tape, center the body on the base, and glue it in place. Fill any gaps at the edges and corners with wood filler. Add the feet, knob, and face decorations (see step 5 on page 139). Lightly sand the entire assembly, then apply a coat of primer. When the primer is dry, paint the clock and let it dry. (We used Light Willow Americana Satin paint by DecoArt, then sponged on a yellow glaze.) Install the clock movement.*

FRAMED VASES

Frames give added importance to everything, even flowers.

1▸ Cut the plywood pieces as indicated in the drawing below. Stack the pieces for the sides of the shadow box and drill a ⅛" (3 mm) hole through both. Assemble the shadow box, using wire brads and glue. Clamp the box together until the glue dries.

2▸ Run a bead of construction adhesive along the top edge of the shadow box and position it on the back of the frame. Let the adhesive dry, then paint or stain the outside of the finished box as you wish.

3▸ Cut the backing from ¼" (6 mm) acid-free foam board. Use spray fixative to secure handmade paper to the backing and to the inside faces of the shadow box. Form silver solder into loops for the vase holders; thread one end through each side of the shadow box and bend an angle to hold it in place. Add test tubes or small, cylindrical vases and fresh or silk flowers.

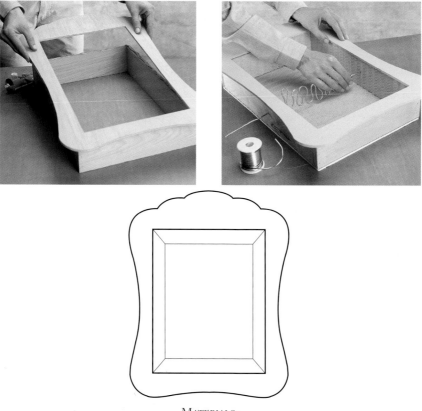

MATERIALS:

• ¼" (6 MM) PLYWOOD • WOOD GLUE • WIRE BRADS • CONSTRUCTION ADHESIVE • PAINT OR STAIN • FOAM BOARD • SPRAY FIXATIVE • SILVER SOLDER • TEST TUBES OR VASES • FRESH OR SILK FLOWERS • HANDMADE PAPER

HANGING FLOWERS

Old-fashioned enamel buckets find new life as flowerpots.

1 Poke some holes in a cake tin, using an awl or nail set. Set the tin (upside down) into the bottom of each bucket. Cover each tin with a piece of landscape fabric and a 2" (5 cm) layer of pea gravel. Add lightweight potting soil and plants.

2 Install a hook in the ceiling—use hardware designed to hold at least 25 pounds (11 kg), and be sure you hit a joist. Drill a hole about ½" (12 mm) from each end of a 13" (33 cm) piece of a hardwood 1 × 2 (2.5 × 5 cm). Run a rope around the pulley and thread one end through each hole in the board. Suspend the pulley from a chain attached to the hook, then tie one end of the rope to each bucket.

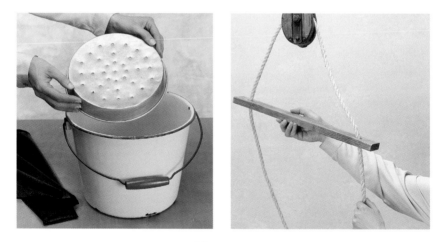

MATERIALS:

• CAKE TINS (2) • BUCKETS (2) • LANDSCAPE FABRIC • PEA GRAVEL • POTTING SOIL • PLANTS
• CEILING HOOK • 1 × 2 (2.5 × 5 CM) HARDWOOD • PULLEY • ROPE • CHAIN

SUSPENDED VASES

Flexible aluminum tubing and silver solder take the shapes of vases and bottles.

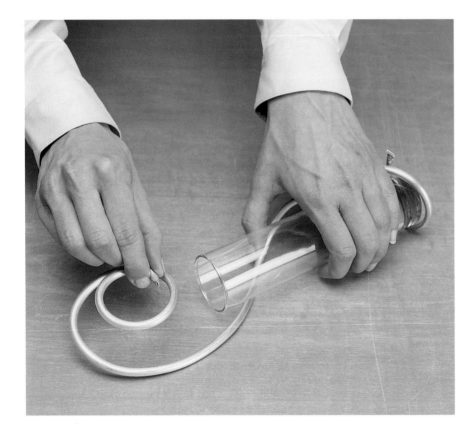

Aluminum Tubing: Shape ¼" (6 mm) aluminum tubing around a tall, cylindrical vase. Be sure the shaped tubing forms a base that will support the weight of the vase. At the top of the vase, form a graceful hanging loop. Hang the vase from a small crystal knob or other decorative hanger.

Silver Solder: Use wooden dowels of various sizes to shape silver solder into spirals and decorative shapes. Drape a loop of solder over the top of the bottle to act as a hanging loop; use loops of solder or wire to hold the hanging loop in place. Add wire accents or decorative beads.

MATERIALS:
• ALUMINUM TUBING • VASE
• SILVER SOLDER • DOWELS • BOTTLES
• SMALL CRYSTAL DOORKNOB

BIRCH BARK VASE

Surrounding a tall tin can and wildflowers, birch bark graces rustic settings.

1▷ Peel the bark from the birch log or select an appropriate piece. (See page 178 for information on peeling birch bark.) If necessary, soak the bark in water until it's flexible. Wrap the bark around the tin can and mark it for cutting. Trim the bark to size, using a utility knife. On both sides of the seam, ¾" (19.1 mm) from the edge, mark and punch evenly spaced holes, approximately ¾" apart. Hot glue a 1¼" (3.18 cm) strip of bark, wrong-side out, to the top of the rectangle, then punch evenly spaced holes ¾" (19.1 mm) from the top edge, through both layers of bark.

2▷ Run a bead of hot glue around the back of the bark, wrap it around the tin can, and use rubber bands to hold it in place. Form the vine into a circle and clip it to the top edge. Tie a piece of lacing to the vine, and thread the lacing through the first hole. Wrap the lacing over the vine and up through the holes in the bark, all the way around the can. At the joint, wrap the lacing to the inside and knot it. At the seam, thread the lacing through the prepunched holes, alternating from one side to the other. At the end of the seam, bring the lacing to the wrong side of the bark and knot it.

MATERIALS:

• TIN CAN, 64-OUNCE (1.9-L) SIZE • BIRCH LOG OR PIECES OF BARK • LEATHER LACING OR RAFFIA
• HOLE PUNCH • FLEXIBLE VINE OR WILLOW TWIG, AT LEAST 18" (45.72 CM) LONG • HOT GLUE

WATERING CAN

A flower-market can plus some plumbing pipe and fittings
equals an artistic watering can.

1 *Cut 36" (90 cm) of copper tubing; use a rubber mallet to flatten the first 4" (10 cm) of one end. Clamp the flattened end to a #12 garden pail and form a circle. Refine the circle into a handle that fits the flower can. Now, cut away the lower three-quarters of a ½" (12 mm) tee fitting, then drill a ⅛" (3 mm) hole in each remaining tab. Also drill two ⅛" (3 mm) holes at the flattened end of the handle.*

2 *Form an open "S" shape from a 30"*
(75 cm) piece of copper tubing; trim one end square and the other at an angle—the final result should be 24" (60 cm) long. Solder a ½" (12 mm) brass flare fitting to the square-cut end. Fold a 32" (80 cm) piece of 8-gauge (4 mm) copper wire in half, maintaining a 1" (25 mm) arc at the fold. On the can, draw two reference lines opposite each other and 90° from the seam. At one line, mark and drill a ½" (12 mm) hole ¾" (19 mm) up from the bottom of the can. Then drill four ³⁄₁₆" (5 mm) holes ⅜" (9 mm) down from the rim and ½" (12 mm) on either side of the remaining reference line.

3 *Assemble the handle and fittings; drill holes and attach the handle with ⅛" (3 mm) aluminum rivets. Lightly solder the handle and fittings in place. Thread the ends of the stay through the holes and make a 90° bend ⅜" (9 mm) from the end of each. Rest the angled end of the spout in the loop of the stay and thread the other end through the can; use a ring nut and silicone sealant to secure it. Lightly solder the point where the spout and the stay meet. From the inside, seal all rivet locations with silicone.*

MATERIALS:
- COPPER TUBING • GARDEN PAIL
- ¼" (6 MM) BRASS FLARE FITTING
- COPPER WIRE • ALUMINUM RIVETS
- RING NUT • SILICONE SEALANT
- ½" (12 MM) TEE FITTING

CEILING TILE PLANTER

Tin ceiling panels convert a simple wooden box into a striking planter.

1 *Assemble 2 × 2 (5 × 5 cm) frames as shown in the illustration. Secure plywood to each frame, using glue and wood screws.*

2 *Join the frames into a box, and then add plywood to the bottom.*

3 *Run several beads of construction adhesive across the backs of the ceiling tiles, and then clamp them in place. Cut the 1 × 3s (2.5 × 7.5 cm) and corner trim; paint the 1 × 3s (2.5 × 7.5 cm), the corner trim, and the 2 × 2 (5 × 5 cm) at the top of each frame to match or complement your ceiling tiles. Drill pilot holes and nail the 1 × 3s (2.5 × 7.5 cm) to the bottom of the planter; add the corner trim in the same way.*

MATERIALS:

• TIN CEILING TILE • 2 × 2s (5 × 5 CM) • ¼" (6 MM) PLYWOOD
• 1 × 3s (2.5 × 7.5 CM) • CONSTRUCTION ADHESIVE • WOOD GLUE
• 2½" (6 CM) WOOD SCREWS • PAINT OR STAIN • CORNER TRIM

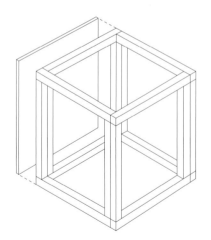

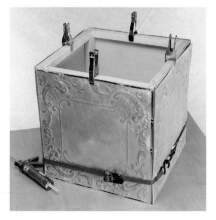

SPIRAL TOPIARY

With masking tape, a pair of pruners, and a basic shrub, you can shape a shrub into an exquisite topiary.

1 Choose a full, cone-shaped conifer. (We used a Dwarf Alberta Spruce, Picea glauco "Conica.") Wind tape around the tree in a spiral. The tape will be a cutting guide, and the goal is to divide the tree into three sections that get thicker toward the base.

2 Starting at the top, cut back the branches just above and below the tape. Work slowly and clip only a little at a time until you see the spiral begin to take shape.

3 Remove the tape. Trim the remaining branches to reinforce the shape and create smooth, round edges for the spiral.

Note: A topiary such as this can live in a bright room for three to four weeks at a time, but then it will need to spend some time outdoors. While it's indoors, mist it often and water it regularly. Prune your topiary each spring. Protect it from strong sunlight for its first few weeks and after each touch-up.

MATERIALS:

• CONIFER • MASKING TAPE

FRAMES

Display favorite photos or prints in fabulous frames.

Beadboard Frame

MATERIALS:

• BEADBOARD • ¼" HARDBOARD • BRADS • WOOD GLUE • PRIMER • LATEX PAINT
• 7 × 13½" GLASS • RETAINER CLIPS • HANGING HARDWARE AND WIRE

1 *Cut a piece of beadboard, 10 × 17" (255 × 435 mm). On the back of the beadboard, mark three 3 × 5" (75 × 125 mm) rectangles, centered on the beadboard and 2" (50 mm) apart from one another. Drill a small hole in one corner of each marked rectangle. For each, slip the blade of a jig-saw into the hole, and cut along the marked lines. If necessary, use a straightedge and a utility knife to clean up the cuts.*

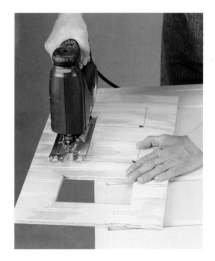

2 Cut a 9 × 15½" (230 × 395 mm) piece of hardboard, then cut a 7 × 13½" (205 × 355 mm) piece from the middle, leaving a 1"-wide (25 mm) rectangle. Center this on the back of the frame; glue and tack it in place. Prime and paint the frame and let it dry. Set the glass in place. Tape the photos or prints to a 7 × 13½" piece of hardboard. Set the backing into the frame and attach four retainer clips to hold it in place. Add hanging hardware.

Molding Compound Frame

MATERIALS:
- ½" (12 MM) MDF • HARD MOLDING COMPOUND
- STAR TIP AND DISPOSABLE CAKE DECORATING BAGS • PRIMER
- SPRAY PAINT • ANTIQUING GLAZE • 5¼ × 7¼" (134 × 184 MM) GLASS
- ¼" (6 MM) HARDBOARD • GLAZING POINTS • HANGING HARDWARE

1 Cut an 8 × 10" (203 × 254 mm) rectangle of MDF, and mark a 4½ × 6½" (115 × 165 mm) rectangle centered within. Drill a hole at each corner, and use a jigsaw to cut out this center rectangle. If necessary, use a hammer and chisel to clean up the edges of the cutout. On the back, use a ⅜" (10 mm) straight bit to rout a channel at the edges of the cutout. Apply a coat of primer to all sides and edges of the frame, and let it dry thoroughly. Across the front, use a straightedge to draw straight lines, ½" (12 mm) apart. Fill the decorating bag with molding compound, and add a star tip. Pipe stars along each marked line, as close to

one another as possible. Let the compound dry for several hours. Working on one edge at a time, cover the edges of the frame with rows of stars. Let the compound dry for 48 hours.

2 Apply two coats of spray paint, letting the paint dry between coats. When the final coat is dry, brush antiquing glaze over the surface, then wipe away the excess with a

Embellished Frame

1 Select two inexpensive frames that complement one another. One must be larger than the other. (We bought these at a garage sale for 50 cents each.) Set one frame inside the other, and mark the corners of the smaller frame onto the larger one. Using a miter saw, cut the larger frame at the marked spots. It's best to err on the side of generosity, if at all. If the frame's slightly too large, you can trim it, but if it's too small, there's no way to make it work. Position the frame pieces, add wood glue to the joints, and secure them with a strap clamp. When the glue is dry, remove the clamp, and turn the frame over. Glue the smaller frame to the back of the larger one and let it dry. Fill any gaps with paintable latex caulk. Apply a coat of latex primer or pigmented shellac to the frame.

2 Assemble a disposable cake decorating bag with a coupler and leaf tip. Fill the bag with molding compound, and knead the compound to eliminate air pockets so it will flow smoothly. Pipe two leaves at each corner of the frame; switch to a beading tip and pipe a row of beading in a recess. (You may want to practice on paper first.) Let the compound dry thoroughly. Spray a coat of silver paint onto the frame and let it dry. If necessary, add a second coat. Apply a coat of antiquing glaze and let it set for a few minutes. Using a clean, dry cloth, remove the excess glaze. Leave enough glaze to enhance the frame's details. When the finish is dry, replace the original glass, backing, and hardware from the smaller frame.

clean cloth. Attach the hanging hardware on the back of the frame. Add glass, a photo or print, and a 5¼ × 7¼" piece of hardboard. Insert glazing points to hold the backing and glass in place.

MATERIALS:
• INEXPENSIVE FRAMES (2) • WOOD GLUE • PAINTABLE LATEX CAULK
• LEAF AND BEADING TIPS • DISPOSABLE CAKE DECORATING BAGS
• HARD MOLDING COMPOUND • PRIMER • SPRAY PAINT
• ANTIQUING GLAZE

RECLAIMED LUMBER FRAME

Discarded pallets are an excellent source of weathered lumber.

1 *Cut a length of lumber that will accommodate the frame you plan to make. Using a router and a piloted rabbet bit set at ¼" (6 mm), cut a rabbet down the length of the wood, along what will be the frame's inside edge.*

2 *Cut four pieces, mitering the ends at 45°. Apply polyurethane glue to the edges and assemble the joints. Band the frame together while the glue dries.*

3 *Cut six circles of ¼" (6 mm) plywood, using a 1" (2.5 cm) hole saw. Use a 1" (2.5 cm) spade bit to drill two holes centered along each joint. Glue one plywood circle into each hole to secure the joints.*

MATERIALS:

• SALVAGED LUMBER • POLYURETHANE GLUE • SCRAP PLYWOOD

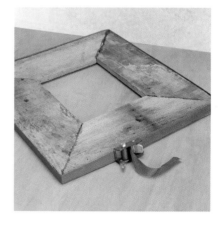

$\mathcal{T}$ECHNIQUES

We hope the projects in this book have lit your creative fires and inspired you to make use of old materials in new ways. As we designed the projects and described construction processes, our main goal was to make sure everyday people could actually do the things we suggested. As you look through these pages, we hope you'll think, "Hey, I can do that!"

By and large, the techniques necessary for these projects are a matter of common sense. Still, it's useful to think about the best ways to clean vintage fabrics or maintain worn finishes, for example, before you make a mistake that can't be undone. And lamp wiring—although extremely simple—may be something you have not tried before. No problem. In the next few pages, you'll find ideas and suggestions that will help you with the projects in the book.

If a project requires tools or materials you haven't used before, take some time to become familiar with them. If it's possible, practice with scrap materials before you start work on the project itself—it will be well worth your time.

If you have questions after reading this chapter, most hardware stores and home centers have staff members who are happy to answer questions.

Most of all, relax. Have fun. You really can do this.

When you get your treasures home, cleaning and repairing them usually is the first order of the day. Not so fast! Original finishes add enormously to the value of a piece, and even aggressive cleaning can damage them. Certain types of repairs can drastically reduce the value of antiques. It's easy to alter an item and impossible to return it to its original condition, so think carefully before you act. Consult an expert if you have doubts or questions. If you bought the piece from a knowledgeable antiques dealer, start there. If you have reason to believe the piece might be especially valuable, talk to an appraiser or a conservator.

Throughout this chapter, we're going to talk about the kinds of materials we use in the projects to come—old doors, wood chairs, chests, or cabinets—run-of-the-mill flea market finds that have appeal based on their character rather than their historical or monetary value. We'll show you how to clean, repair, and adapt items such as these. If you've decided to refinish or restore an antique, first do some research. Bookstores and libraries offer many fine books on the subject.

CLEANING PAINTED FINISHES

Note: Paint from before 1978 is very likely to contain lead. If you suspect you're dealing with lead paint, use proper precautions, and by all means, keep these pieces well out of the reach of children.

Wash painted surfaces with a solution of equal parts of vinegar and water, and a soft cloth; remove flaking paint. To remove stubborn stains, rub the surface gently with a scouring pad; use an old toothbrush in small areas.

Popular opinion seems to be divided about waxing painted pieces. Some experts recommend it and others advise against the idea. I'm not an expert, but I've waxed many painted pieces and have never had a reason to regret it. If you decide to wax a painted surface, use beeswax and a light touch. With a soft, lint-free cloth, rub the wax onto the surface; buff the wax with a clean cloth. Adding another coat or two will produce a soft luster.

In some cases, a clear finish is best. After cleaning the piece, use a sponge applicator or a natural-bristle paintbrush to apply a clear acrylic finish. Add three coats, allowing plenty of drying time in between.

CLEANING FINISHED WOOD

The most important ingredient for cleaning wood is common sense. Cleaning a rustic piece that's been in a barn for 30 years is simple. A fine piece that has a shellacked or lacquered finish requires a different approach.

Let's start with the rustics. This is a look I love: Old and cruddy is my thing, but I don't want to bring dirt into my house, and I don't imagine you do, either. In good weather, start outside with a hose, a soft scrub brush, and some mild soap and water. If that's not possible, work at a utility sink or in a large bucket.

When the weather permits, let the piece dry outdoors in the sun, to give it a chance to air out and lose any musty odor it might have. If a musty odor persists, wash the piece again with a weak bleach-and-water solution. Rinse the wood thoroughly with a vinegar solution to neutralize the bleach and then with water to remove any residue. Let the piece dry overnight.

Apply a light coat of beeswax and buff it with a clean, soft, lint-free cloth; add two more coats. To maintain this finish, wax the piece whenever the wood looks dry or when a drop of water won't bead up on the surface.

Shellacked or lacquered finishes require more careful handling. Wash these pieces with a soft cloth and a weak vinegar-and-water solution. On stubborn spots you can use an old, soft toothbrush if necessary.

REPAIRING SURFACE FLAWS

Most of the time, it's best to leave minor imperfections exactly as they are—they provide character. But there are some situations where it makes sense to repair minor surface flaws, and it's usually fairly easy to do.

Shallow dents can be raised with water or steam. Start by applying a few drops of distilled water into the dent; let the water soak in. In most cases, the dented wood will swell back to its original shape. If not, place a wet rag directly over the dent; touch the rag with the tip of a hot iron. The resulting steam often causes the wood to swell back into shape. If that fails, fill the dent with wood putty.

Minor scratches or dents can be filled with wood putty. To get rid of debris that could keep the putty from bonding, clean out the damaged area with a pointed scraper, such as a modeling tool. If the flaw is very shallow, make it a little deeper. Next, use a putty knife to fill the damaged area with stainable wood putty. Scrape away the excess, leaving the putty just slightly above the surface of the wood. When the putty is dry, sand the area until the putty is level with the wood surface. To blend the repair into the area, color the putty with stain or a touch-up marker that matches the color of the wood.

Water damage or contact with metal sometimes creates black stains on wood. These stains can be removed with a mixture of oxalic acid crystals and distilled water. Paint the solution onto the stain and let it soak in. Rinse and repeat as necessary.

Chlorine bleach will remove many spot stains. Working in an area with good ventilation, brush undiluted bleach onto the stain and wait 20 minutes. To help activate the bleach, set the workpiece out in direct sunlight. Rinse the bleach with water and reapply as necessary. As soon as you're finished, neutralize the bleach: Wipe white vinegar onto the area and then rinse it immediately with water.

REGLUING VENEERS

Making basic veneer repairs, such as regluing loose or blistered veneer, is a fairly simple job. More complicated repairs involving patching should be left to professionals.

Before deciding to reglue loose veneer, try using heat to renew the bond. Cover the loosened veneer with a damp cloth; press the cloth with a household iron set on low. Keep the iron moving—don't leave it in place for more than a few seconds. Wait for the veneer glue to liquefy, then remove the iron and the cloth. Before the glue rehardens, roll the area with a seam roller. Set a weight such as a heavy book on the area as it cools.

If ironing doesn't work, reglue the loose spots. Use a putty or palette knife to lift the veneer so you can clean below it with a brush. Veneer is fragile—be careful not to tear it. If there's glue on the surface, scrub it with a cotton swab dipped in hot vinegar. Next, use a cotton swab or a glue injector to squeeze glue under the veneer. Cover the area with waxed paper and a clamping block and clamp the area until the glue dries. Remove the clamp and carefully scrape away any excess glue with a chisel.

Missing sections of veneer are difficult to repair. If you still have the missing piece and it's intact, it can be reglued in the manner described above. If you don't have the pieces, get professional help. Cutting and gluing down new veneer patches is a job that requires finesse and experience.

Blistered veneer can be repaired in much the same way as loose veneer. Start by using a craft knife to slice the blister along the grain. Use a small brush to clean out any debris, then slip a thin spacer under the veneer. Inject carpenter's glue into the area, roll the blister with a seam roller, and cover the area with waxed paper. Clamp or weight the loose veneer down until the glue dries. If the veneer overlaps at the seam, slice away the excess, using a craft knife and a straightedge.

REPAIRING JOINTS & SPLITS

Loose joints and split parts, common structural problems, usually can be corrected by gluing and reinforcing the joints.

Use wood sweller to tighten loose joints on parts that don't support much weight, such as interior spindles on a chair. Just squirt the wood sweller into the joint and let it sit—the wood in the joint will swell and tighten.

To repair a split spindle, start by cleaning debris and splinters from the pieces so the mating surfaces fit tightly. Apply glue to the mating surfaces, wrap the spindle with waxed paper, then press the parts together. Slip hose clamps over the repair, spaced every 3 to 4" (7 to 10 cm); tighten the clamps. Let the glue dry, remove the clamps and paper, and scrape away the excess glue with a chisel.

Structural joints that need to support weight can be repaired with two-part epoxy. Drill at least two $\frac{3}{16}$"-diameter (5 mm) holes per joint. Using a self-mixing injector, deliver two-part epoxy glue into each hole. The epoxy will harden into "nails" that will reinforce the joints.

PATCHING DAMAGED WOOD

We use doors in several projects throughout the book, and although interesting doors are easy to find, they're sometimes damaged by rot—especially screen doors, which are exposed to the elements. You may also find this kind of damage in other pieces you'd like to use. It can be remedied with epoxy wood filler, which can be molded and shaped easily, and readily accepts paint or stain.

Start by removing the damaged wood with a chisel or utility knife. (Wear eye protection while chiseling wood.) Build simple wood forms as needed to establish boundaries for the repair. Coat the forms with wax or oil so the filler won't stick to them.

Mix and apply the wood filler, according to package instructions. Use a putty knife or trowel to shape the repair area to match the existing contours. Let the filler harden completely.

Remove the forms and lightly sand the hardened filler. Use a light hand—oversanding closes the filler's pores and makes it difficult to stain. Paint or stain the wood to match the existing finish.

CLEANING METAL, LEATHER & CANVAS

As copper, brass, and bronze age, they develop a patina, called *verdigris*, in various shades of green, blue, and brown. Iron, tin, and other metals develop a layer of oxidation known as rust. Both verdigris and rust add an interesting range of colors and textures to an old piece.

To remove rust from metal, use fine steel wool and lubricant oil, such as WD-40®. Scour carefully, working in circles. When you're finished, wipe the area with mineral spirits to remove the oil residue. Let the area dry, then wipe it again with a clean cloth.

To clean and preserve a surface covered with rust or verdigris, wash the piece with a 1:1 vinegar-and-water solution and let it dry.

In either case, apply a light coat of clear acrylic sealer and let that dry. Add three or four coats of sealer, letting it dry between coats. If you want to preserve the current level of oxidation on an iron piece, use a rust-inhibiting sealer.

Note: Sealing a weathered surface may darken the patina's color somewhat.

Use Liquid Steel filler to patch any holes or tears in tin. Badly damaged areas can be replaced: Cut away the old tin, using tin snips, and nail on new pieces. Use Liquid Steel filler to bridge the ridge between the old tin and the patch. If necessary, touch up the area with rust-inhibiting metal primer and enamel paint.

Use saddle soap and a soft rag to clean leather. Let the leather dry, then polish it with a leather dressing, such as mink oil. Use all-purpose cement to reglue any tears.

Scrub canvas gently, using a brush and mild soap. Reglue any loose areas, using wood glue diluted with an equal amount of water.

CLEANING & RESTORING LINENS

In some ways, textiles carry their stories more than other old pieces. Stains, wear, and mending or signs of alterations give us clues about the people who owned and used these things. Gentle cleaning is important—it protects fibers and prevents deterioration—but it's not always necessary or even a good idea to remove every trace of the history.

When shopping for old textiles, look for pieces in good condition. If you're planning to cut apart a piece to use the fabric in a decorating project, you may be able to work around stains, holes, or weak areas. Remember that it may not be possible to remove stains, and in the process of trying, you may even cause the fabric to disintegrate further.

Old silks are likely to be weighted with metallic salts, lead, or arsenic; handling them can be hazardous. Old silk is extremely fragile, and when torn, it releases harmful fibers.

Fabric becomes even more fragile when wet. Before cleaning old garments and quilts, repair any open seams and reinforce areas around holes or weak spots. It's a good idea to stitch around the outer edges of unfinished pieces, such as needlepoint canvases, quilt tops, or individual quilt blocks, but it isn't necessary to stitch around the selvages of tapestries.

Test the stability of the dyes before washing a textile. Remove yarns of each color or a small piece of fabric from a seam allowance or edge. Lay the pieces on white cotton and press them with a warm steam iron; let them dry for 10 minutes. If dye bleeds onto the white fabric, dry clean the textile instead of washing it.

If it's necessary to dry clean a fragile textile, take it to a dry cleaner who uses the flat dry-cleaning method, which creates less abrasion than the tumble method.

Wash a piece of fiberglass screening and bind the edges with tape. Place the screening in the bottom of a laundry sink or bathtub. Fill the tub with lukewarm or cool water and a small amount of a gentle soap.

Put especially fragile items in a pillowcase or mesh bag before washing them; lay the textile in soapy water and press against it with the palm of your hand rather than agitating or wringing it. For heavily soiled items, change the washing solution often. Rinse several times; make sure you remove all traces of soap residue. Use distilled water for the final rinse.

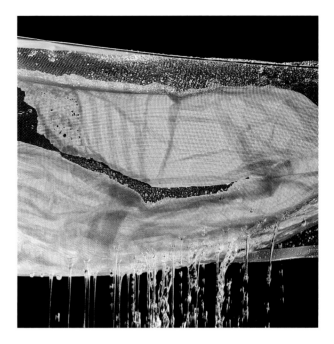

Lift the screening from the bottom of the tub, bringing the fabric along with it. Roll the laundered textile in a white towel to remove the excess moisture; lay the piece flat and pat it into its original shape. Let the fabric air dry only until it's slightly damp. (Directing a fan toward it speeds up the process.)

Iron the piece while the fabric's still damp—when fabric dries completely, it temporarily loses its natural moisture and becomes brittle. And when you iron vintage linens, don't use steam or starch. Steam can bring stains to the surface, and starch can attract pests over time.

To clean vintage lace or doilies, rub a thick paste of salt and white vinegar into spots, using a toothbrush. Next, soak the pieces for an hour or so in a 3:1 solution of water and vinegar. Rinse thoroughly until clean.

Drying white linens in the sun helps to naturally bleach and brighten them.

To avoid mildew, make sure linens are clean before you put them away; keep them in dry, well-ventilated cabinets or closets. Don't store vintage linens in plastic bags—air flow helps the fibers breathe. Lining the shelves or drawers helps reduce exposure to wood fumes, which can cause premature yellowing.

PAINTING

The keys to every good paint job are preparation and patience. This is true whether you're painting the exterior of a house or a tiny bedside table. For these projects, start by lightly sanding the piece, then removing the dust with a tack cloth. Next, apply a coat of primer—sometimes water-based primer and other times pigmented shellac. (The list of materials with each project will guide you.) Let the primer dry, according to the manufacturer's instructions.

The next step in the process is to apply the base coat. Most of the time, this requires two coats. Again, be sure to let the paint dry thoroughly between coats, and add coats until you have a uniform layer of color. When the paint's completely dry, lightly smooth it with fine sandpaper.

For glazing, you can use premixed glaze or combine paint and paint extender in a ratio of 1:1 to create one.

Checkerboard: Glaze the frame and molding, and then the board, as directed on page 134. It's best to add the glaze in layers rather than try to apply too much at one time. To build up layers, let the first coat dry for 48 hours, then repeat.

Cut a piece of tagboard, 18½ × 18½" (47 cm × 47 cm). Draw a 12 × 12" (30.48 cm × 30.48 cm) square, centered on the tagboard (3¼" [8.25 cm] from each edge), then draw a 1½" (3.81 cm) grid within that 12" square. Use a metal straightedge and a razor knife to cut out every other square.

Set the stencil on the board and use a 1" (2.54 cm) brush to apply black glaze to the open squares, moving the brush in the same direction for each stroke. Remove the stencil and let the glaze dry thoroughly. Turn the stencil

180° and paint the remaining squares of the checkerboard. Again, add layers of glaze if necessary to make the squares dark enough.

Spatter the entire piece as described below.

Fish Headboard: Prime and paint the headboard. When the paint's completely dry, apply a coat of glaze and let it set for about five minutes. Using a damp sponge, strategically remove some of the glaze. Let the base color clearly show through in areas where natural wear patterns would occur, such as the contour of the top and the edges near the posts. (Refer to page 174 for information on building up layers of glaze.)

Take special care when working on the textured areas of the fish. The damp sponge will wick glaze from the surface, and the glaze will naturally seek the recesses. This works just fine, because the point is to emphasize the texture of the fish.

When the glaze is completely dry, add spatters. To do this, dip an old toothbrush in glaze and pat it on paper towels until it's nearly dry. Holding the toothbrush about 3" (7.62 cm) from the surface, slowly scrape your thumbnail across the bristles. Move your hand in a straight line, spattering one area of the headboard at a time. If the speckles are too large, there's too much paint on the toothbrush; pat it on the paper towels again. If they're too fine, you need a little more paint on the brush.

DRILLING HOLES IN CHINA

The first thing you need to do for a project like the teacup lamp is drill holes in the pieces. Many lighting stores and glass supply stores offer this service, but you certainly can do it yourself.

If you have a drill press and a hollow, circular diamond drill bit, use them. If not, you need a drill, a glass and tile bit, and some mineral spirits. If you need a large hole, start with a small bit; gradually enlarge the hole by redrilling with increasingly larger bits.

To drill a hole in a plate, put an X of masking tape on the front, at the center of the plate. Pour mineral spirits into the plate and begin drilling. Drill slowly and keep the bit perpendicular to the saucer. (The mineral spirits act as a lubricant and keep the saucer cool as the drill works its way through the ceramic.)

To drill a hole in a cup, pitcher, or jar, mark the center with masking tape, then put the piece upside down in a bucket of sand. Slowly drill the hole as described above—the sand will support the piece and make it easier to drill the hole without cracking or otherwise damaging it.

HARVESTING FRESH WOOD

If you have wooded areas on your property, you can gather twigs and branches from your own trees. If not, contact builders to see if they'll let you gather wood on property that's scheduled to be cleared. Or visit a brush recycling center. Tim's even been known to stop at commercial construction sites and ask for permission to scavenge through their brush piles. People sometimes laugh, but they rarely refuse.

Many kinds of wood will work for building twig furniture. Often the shape and diameter of the branches are more important than the variety of the tree. For many pieces, it's best to use freshly cut wood—it's easier to work with, and as the wood dries, it shrinks around the nails, which results in sturdier construction.

As you scout for branches, consider the shapes you're trying to create and choose accordingly. Straight pieces are often the best choices, but offshoots and curves will give your pieces dramatic flair. Select branches and twigs that aren't infested with insects, and protect living trees by using sharp cutting tools; ripping or tearing branches could kill small trees.

HARVESTING SEASONED WOOD

Some projects, such as the birch tree table on pages 60 and 61 and the log ottoman on pages 72 and 73, require well-seasoned logs. If you're going to cut down a tree, look for one that has been dead for at least one season—the wood should be dry, but not rotten or brittle. If you're harvesting in winter, inspect the tree for new growth buds. If there are no buds, the tree is dead. Keep in mind that most wood-eating insects feed on dead trees. Carefully inspect branches for insects or larvae, and avoid wood from infested trees.

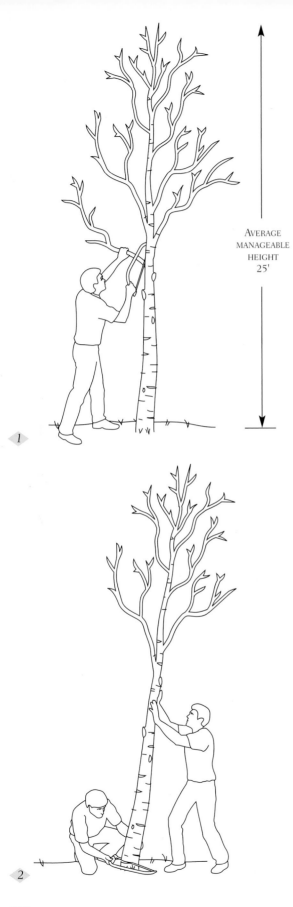

AVERAGE
MANAGEABLE
HEIGHT
25'

1

2

Think about the project you have in mind and, if possible, select one tree that will yield all the material you'll need. The tree should be manageable, however—usually no taller than 25 ft. (7.62 m).

Cut away the lower branches first. Have someone hold the tree while you cut approximately ¾ of the way through its trunk. Then work together to ease the tree down gently, preserving the upper portions.

If possible, store the harvested wood indoors, to avoid attracting insects. When you're ready to use it, inspect the wood again. If you find tiny holes or other evidence of insects, treat the wood with a safe garden insecticide before beginning your projects.

STRIPPING BIRCH BARK

Choose well-seasoned logs that are at least 4" (10.16 cm) in diameter. Smaller logs are more difficult to strip, they yield less bark, and the bark you do get is cupped and resistant to being reshaped.

Use a straightedge and a utility knife to make a cut along the length of a birch log. Cut all the way through the layers of bark and into the pulp. Starting at one end, use a wide chisel to pry the bark away from the log. When enough bark is loosened, switch to a putty knife or paint scraper, and completely remove the bark from the log. Separate the base layers of the bark from the outer layers to produce a thin, pliable material.

When using the bark, position it to take advantage of its natural shape.

MAKING TWIG FURNITURE

Before you start nailing branches together, drill pilot holes through the top branch and into the bottom one. Use a drill bit that's slightly smaller than the diameter of the nail, such as a ³⁄₃₂" (2.4 mm) bit for 6d (5.08 cm) nails and a ³⁄₆₄" (1.2 mm) bit for 4d (3.81 cm) nails. Make the pilot hole approximately ¾ of the length of the nail you will be using. If you have trouble getting pieces to stay in position while you drill or nail, temporarily lash them together with string or raffia.

Flathead galvanized nails work well for most joints. The flat heads hold joints firmly; galvanization keeps them from rusting in either green or seasoned wood. The size of nails used depends on the diameter of the branches you're joining. If the nails are too large, they may split the twigs as they dry. Keep an assortment of nails handy as you work. For each joint, select nails that are slightly shorter than the combined thickness of the pieces you're joining.

When a joint is described as a *butt joint*, one piece is to fit flush against the other to form the joint. If *overlap construction* is used, one piece sits over an adjoining piece or pieces to form the joint.

When a project is complete, check all the stretchers, rails, and connecting pieces. Turn the project upside down and try to wiggle the joints. If a joint wobbles at all, drill more pilot holes and add nails until the joint is stable. At a minimum, each joint should have one nail driven straight through both pieces and another at each side, driven at angles (toenailed) into the joint.

After a piece of twig furniture has cured for several weeks, apply exterior wood sealer or a clear acrylic finish. Cover the entire surface of the wood, especially the cut ends of the branches.

SOLDERING

Soldering, or sweating, joints is much easier than you might imagine. If propane torches intimidate you, try one of the new, compact versions. The smaller size and quieter burn may feel more comfortable while you're learning. To solder a joint, you use a propane torch to heat a copper or brass fitting until it's just hot enough to melt the solder. The heat then draws the solder into the gap between the fitting and the pipe, forming a strong seal.

As with many do-it-yourself tasks, you'll find that good preparation makes everything else much easier. To form a strong joint, the ends of the pipes and the insides of the fittings must be clean and smooth. Soldering copper isn't difficult, but it requires some patience and skill. It's a good idea to practice on scrap pipe before taking on a large project.

The most common mistake beginners make is using too much heat. To avoid this problem, remember that the tip of the torch's inner flame produces the most heat. Direct the flame carefully—solder will flow in the direction the heat has traveled. Heat the pipe just until the flux sizzles; remove the flame and touch the solder to the pipe. The heated pipe will quickly melt the solder.

Plan to work on a heat-resistant surface or on a double layer of 26-gauge (0.5 mm) sheet metal. The sheet metal makes an effective shield, and its reflective quality helps the joints heat evenly.

If a series of pipe and fittings (a run) is involved, dry-fit the entire run before soldering any of the joints. When the run is correctly assembled, take it apart and prepare to solder the joints.

Sand the ends of the pipes with emery cloth and scour the insides of the fittings with a wire brush. Apply a thin layer of water-soluble paste flux to the end of each pipe, using a flux brush. The flux should cover about 1" (25 mm) of the end of the pipe. Insert the pipe into the fitting until the pipe is tight against the fitting socket. Twist the fitting slightly to spread the flux.

When you're ready to solder, unwind 8 to 10" (200 to 250 mm) of solder from the spool. Bend the first 2" (50 mm) of the solder to a 90° angle.

Light the torch and adjust the valve until the inner portion of the flame is 1 to 2" (25 to 50 mm) long. Hold the flame tip against the middle of the fitting for four to five seconds or until the flux begins to sizzle. Heat the other side of the joint, distributing the heat evenly. Move the flame around the joint in the direction the solder should flow. Touch the solder to the pipe, just below the fitting. If it melts, the joint is hot enough.

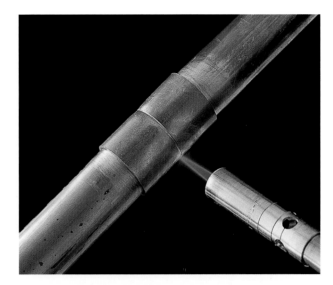

Quickly apply solder along both seams of the fitting, allowing capillary action to draw the liquefied solder into the fitting. When the joint is filled, solder will begin to form droplets on the bottom of the joint. A correctly soldered joint shows a thin bead of silver-colored solder around the lip of the fitting. It typically takes about ½" (12 mm) of solder to fill a joint in ½" (12 mm) pipe.

Note: Always turn off the torch immediately after you've finished soldering; make sure the gas valve is completely closed.

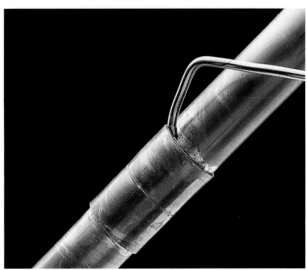

Let the joint sit undisturbed until the solder loses its shiny color—don't touch it before then, as the copper will be quite hot. When the joint is cool enough to touch, wipe away excess flux and solder, using a clean, dry rag. When the joint is cool, check for gaps around the edges. If it's not a good seal, take the joint apart and resolder it.

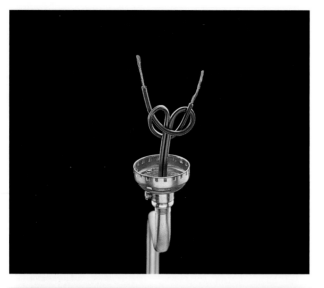

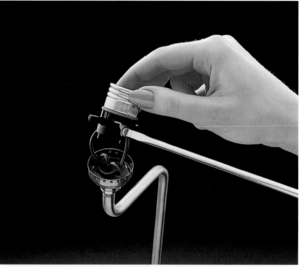

WIRING LAMPS

Wiring a lamp can seem mysterious and complicated unless you realize how few steps it really takes. Basically, all you have to do is thread the lamp cord through the base and up to the socket, and then connect two wires. Very simple—it will probably take less than half an hour to do the whole thing, even the first time. The next time, it will take just a matter of minutes.

Thread the lamp cord through the base and up through the lamp pipe and socket cap. (Many lamp cords are pre-split and the ends are stripped in preparation for wiring. If yours isn't, use a utility knife to split the first 2" [50 mm] of the end of the cord, along the midline of the insulation. Strip about ½ to ¾" [12 to 19 mm] of insulation from the ends of the wires.)

Tie an underwriter's knot by forming an overhand loop with one wire and an underhand loop with the remaining wire; insert each wire end through the loop of the other wire.

Loosen the terminal screws on the socket. Look carefully at the insulation on the wires—the insulation on one wire will be rounded and on the other wire it will be ribbed or will have a fine line on it. Loop the wire on the rounded side around the socket's brass screw and tighten the screw. Loop the wire on the other side around the socket's silver screw and tighten the screw.

Adjust the underwriter's knot to fit within the base of the socket cap, then position the socket into the socket cap. Slide the insulating sleeve and outer shell over the socket so the terminal screws are fully covered and any slots are correctly aligned.

Test the lamp; when you're sure it works, press the socket assembly down into the socket cap until the socket locks into place.

PATTERNS

Linoleum Floor Cloth (page 15)—enlarge by 800%

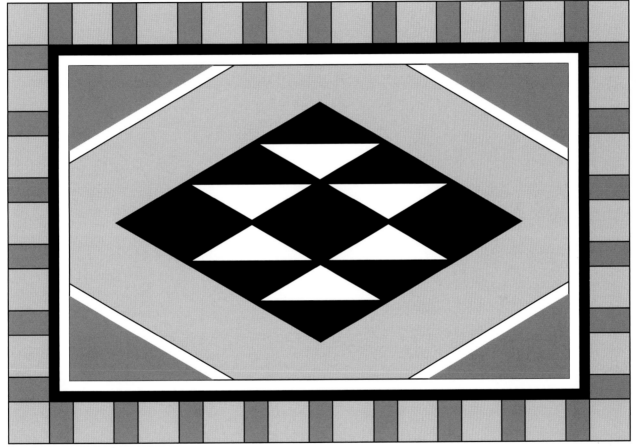

Drop Leaf Table (page 65)—enlarge by 300%

Display Shelf (page 37)

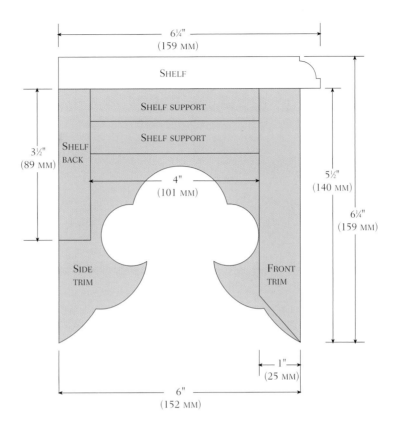

6¼"
(159 ᴍᴍ)

SHELF

SHELF SUPPORT

SHELF SUPPORT

SHELF
BACK

3½"
(89 ᴍᴍ)

4"
(101 ᴍᴍ)

5½"
(140 ᴍᴍ)

6¼"
(159 ᴍᴍ)

SIDE
TRIM

FRONT
TRIM

1"
(25 ᴍᴍ)

6"
(152 ᴍᴍ)

Fish Headboard (page 103)—100% sm; enlarge by 155% lg

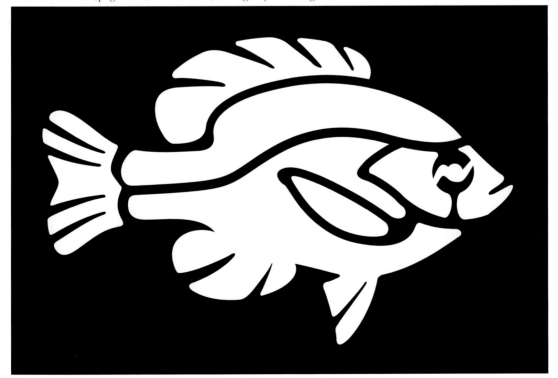

INDEX

RESOURCES

Photo Credits:

© Balthazar Korab, Ltd.: p. 11B

Photo courtesy of Maine Cottage Furniture, Inc, photo by Dennis Welsh: p. 12

© Jerry Pavia: p. 74

Contributors:

We would like to thank the following stores and companies for their generous support:

April Cornell
3565 Galleria
Edina, MN 55435
952-836-0830
www.aprilcornell.com

Crescent Moon
58 S. Hamline (at Grand)
St. Paul, MN 55105
651-690-9630

The Gilded Salvage Antiques
1315 NE Tyler St.
Minneapolis, MN 55413
612-789-1680

Old World Antiques
4911 Excelsior Blvd.
St. Louis Park, MN 55416
952-929-1638

Past Lives
1787 St. Clair Ave.
St. Paul, MN 55105
www.pastlivesinc.com

Smith & Hawken
3564 Galleria
Edina, MN 55435
952-285-1110
www.smithandhawken.com

Squire House Gardens
3390 St. Croix Trail
Afton, MN
651-436-8080
www.squirehousegardens.com

Sticks & Stones Interiors
4000 Minnetonka Blvd.
Minneapolis, MN 55416
952-926-1567

Que Será
3580 Galleria
Edina, MN 55435
952-924-6390

Oh Baby!
3515 Galleria
Edina, MN 55435
952-928-9119

Oh Baby! On the Lake
743 E. Lake Street
Wayzata, MN 55391
952-404-0170

McCoy Pottery Collection
Courtesy of Jeanette Moss McCurdy
Stillwater, MN

Architectural Products by Outwater
22 Passaic Street
Wood-Ridge, NJ 07075
(Locations also in Arizona and Canada)
Free Catalog Request: 1-888-435-4400
www.outwater.com

Land of Oz Bed and Breakfast
N1874 670th Street
Bay City, WI 54723
715-594-3844
www.landofoztouristcottages.com

Eddie Bauer Home Store
Mall of America
230 West Market
Bloomington, MN 55425
952-851-0727
www.eddiebauer.com

Spider Lake Lodge Bed & Breakfast Inn
10472 W. Murphy Blvd.
Hayward, WI 54843
Info & Reservations:
1-800-OLD-WISC
www.haywardlakes.com/spiderlakelodge

Harmon Interiors—Trude Harmon
780 Como Avenue
St. Paul, MN 55103
651-488-2983

Private collection of Susan & Him Wolfe
8 Wolfe Lane
South of Forsythe
Forsythe, MT 59327
406-356-7673

From the Collection of Neal Anderson &
Miriam Buhler
5004 17th Avenue South
Minneapolis, MN 55417
612-729-5913

Dakota Trading Post
Edna Mae Anderson
Alexandria, MN 56308
320-763-3551

Liz Birr
Onahu Log Works
970-669-3004

CREDITS

Creative Publishing international

President/CEO: Ken Fund
Vice President/Publisher: Linda Ball
Vice President/Retail Sales & Marketing:
  Kevin Haas

Copyright © 2005
Creative Publishing international, Inc.
18705 Lake Drive East
Chanhassen, MN 55317
1-800-328-3895
www.creativepub.com
All rights reserved.

Printed in Singapore
10 9 8 7 6 5 4 3 2 1

Library of Congress Cataloging-in-Publication Data

Farris, Jerri.
  Handcrafted projects for your home : 56 make-it-yourself accessories
to personalize your space / by Jerri Farris & Tim Himsel.
    p. cm.
  Includes index.
  ISBN 1-58923-222-4 (soft cover)
  1. Handicraft. 2. House furnishings. I. Himsel, Tim. II. Title.
  TT157.F332 2005
  745.5--dc22

                    2005013649

Executive Editor: Bryan Trandem
Creative Director: Tim Himsel
Project Manager: Tracy Stanley

Authors: Jerri Farris, Tim Himsel
Editor: Thomas Lemmer
Senior Art Director: David Schelitzche
Mac Designer: Jon Simpson
Photo Editor: Julie Caruso
Production Manager: Laura Hokkanen
Photographers: Tate Carlson, Chuck Nields, Andrea Rugg
Scene Shop Carpenter: Randy Austin
Illustrator: Earl Slack

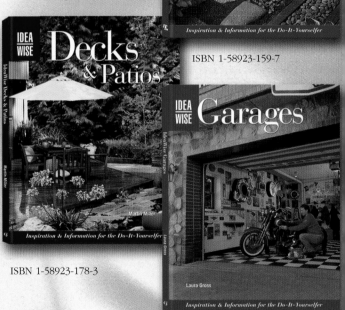